Praise for Alan Loy McGinnis's
THE POWER OF OPTIMISM

"Though I have been an optimist always, Alan McGinnis has shown me in this book how to combine realism with optimism, to the increase of both."
   —*Trammell Crow, founder, The Trammell Crow Company*

"THE POWER OF OPTIMISM can help any pessimist become more optimistic."
   —*Sandra Kulli, president, Kulli Marketing*

"By the time I reached the age of 60, life had taught me that things turn out best for the people who make the best of the way things turn out. This fine book by Dr. Alan Loy McGinnis confirms and enlarges my own belief, and further, gives inspiring examples of how important attitudes are, and just as important, how attitudes are not inherited but can be acquired."
   —*Art Linkletter*

"No mumbo jumbo or psychological jargon here. Dr. McGinnis provides a common sense approach which can help transform your glass from half empty to half full."
   —*Pat Sajak, host, "Wheel of Fortune"*

"McGinnis has really done it this time, given us wisdom, wit, inspiration, and profound truth, and all in one readable book; he gets better and better."
—*Lewis B. Smedes, Ph.D., author of* Forgive and Forget

"I really enjoy this book. If you read it, your attitude will become more positive, your problems smaller; your self-confidence will grow, and your self-doubt disintegrate."
—*Lou Holtz, head football coach, Notre Dame*

"A marvelous, no-nonsense book. It combines realism with optimism and further affords inspiring examples from which we can all learn and benefit."
—*Robert H. Schuller, founder, Crystal Cathedral*

This book could help anyone develop an optimistic attitude. THE POWER OF OPTIMISM is strong, and Dr. McGinnis's tools and examples on achieving it are excellent."
—*Mary Kay Ash, founder, Mary Kay Cosmetics*

"Laser-accurate, timeless wisdom to unlock the power to win within us. The 1990s belong to the practical optimist identified in this important book."
—*Denis Waitley, author of* The Psychology of Winning

"Delightful surprises, full of uplifting insights and meaningful signals to redirect your life."
—*Victor K. Kiam II, CEO, Remington Products*

"The citations about robust optimists such as Winston Churchill, C. S. Lewis, and Thomas Edison are alone worth the price of this latest work by McGinnis."
—*Keith W. Sehnert, M.D., author of* Stress/Unstress

"This is a terrific book. It underlines everything I know about effective leaders—and how. What McGinnis means by 'optimism' is not soft and mushy psychobabble but strong and muscular ways to become an integrated self."
—*Dr. Warren Bennis, Distinguished Professor of Business Administration, USC, author of* On Becoming a Leader

"What a book! Here's education, motivation, and inspiration for anyone interested in developing a blueprint for personal and professional success. An outstanding work filled with strategies and hints to help us all. I highly recommend it."
—*Nido R. Qubein, chairman, Creative Services, Inc.*

"This book packs as much good sense into a small space as anything I've ever read."
—*Rabbi Harold Kushner, author of* When Bad Things Happen to Good People *and* Who Needs God?

"Another outstanding McGinnis book with a powerful message."
—*Stephen T. Bow, CLU, president, CEO, Blue Cross Blue Shield of Kentucky*

"A magnificently helpful book. In my fifteen years on the faculty of a graduate school of psychology, I have seldom read a book that I am as eager to share with those who look to me for insights, enlightenment, and direction."
—*Neil Clark Warren, Ph.D., clinical psychologist*

"This book is splendid. It met all my expectations."
—*Björn-Ingvar Olsson, president, Libris Media, Sweden*

"It is clear that Alan Loy McGinnis possesses a special insight into the human spirit and its need to generate a boldness for living. Those in search of courage or those seeking for handles on how to encourage others are going to love this book."
—*Gordon MacDonald, author of* Ordering Your Private World

"In this book, Alan McGinnis has shared the secret of a happier, more satisfying life through implementation of a forward-thinking, optimistic approach towards life's ups and downs. Using real life examples, this very readable book illustrates the power within each of us to create a positive environment in which to live."
—*Ed Foreman, former U.S. congressman, and currently president of Executive Development Systems*

"Dr. McGinnis speaks to our minds and our hearts in a loving and dynamic way. I highly recommend this book."
—*Zig Ziglar, author of* Closing the Sale

☐ The Power
of *Optimism*

Also by Alan Loy McGinnis

Books:
The Friendship Factor
The Romance Factor
Bringing Out the Best in People
Confidence

Audio Cassette Albums:
How to Get Closer to People You Care For
The Romance Factor
Motivation Without Manipulation
Confidence
The Power of Optimism

☐ The Power
of *Optimism*

Alan Loy McGinnis

1817

Harper & Row Publishers, San Francisco
New York, Grand Rapids, Philadelphia, St. Louis
London, Singapore, Sydney, Tokyo, Toronto

For information on Alan Loy McGinnis's lectures and consulting services write to: Valley Counseling Center, 517 East Wilson, Suite 204, Glendale, CA 91206; or phone: 818-240-9322.

Acknowledgment is made for permission to reprint the following material: Excerpts from *Leadership Is an Art* by Max DePree, copyright © 1987 by Max DePree. Reprinted by permission of Doubleday, a division of Bantam Doubleday Dell Publishing Group, Inc.; from *Beyond Survival* by Gerald L. Coffee, published by G. P. Putnam's Sons, by Captain Gerald Coffee, U.S. Navy (Ret.); from "At 88, Harry Lipsig starts New Firm, Gets New Daughter." Reprinted by permission of the *Wall Street Journal*, © Dow Jones & Company, Inc., 1989. All Rights Reserved Worldwide.

Library of Congress Cataloging-in-Publication Data

McGinnis, Alan Loy.
   The power of optimism / Alan Loy McGinnis.
     p.   cm.
   Includes bibliographical references.

   1. Optimism. 2. Adjustment (Psychology)   I. Title.
BF698.35.O57M24   1990   90–32589
158′.1–dc20   CIP

☐ *Since this is a book about optimism, it is dedicated to the most sensible optimist I know. A positive outlook does not always come naturally for me, but it does for this woman, and much of what I know about the topic has come by watching the way she lives. When we met, many years ago, she had been dealt some tough blows—the sort that leave many people hard and bitter. Although she may have been a little bruised, she certainly was not hard or bitter. Instead she was eager to live and laugh and love again. Her enthusiasm has gradually rubbed off on me over the years, and I continue to admire my wife Diane more than anyone I know.*

Contents

Acknowledgments

At Valley Counseling Center, where I work, my colleagues are always teaching me new things about the practice of psychotherapy, and much of their wisdom has doubtless seeped onto these pages. Dr. Taz Kinney, Tricia Kinney, Melody McKee, Renée Palmer, Séan Smith, and Susan Wade are far more than co-workers. They are valued friends. They have been tolerant when some writing deadline has kept me incommunicado, and they have taken good care of my patients during these absences.

For fifteen years I have met monthly with a group of men who try to keep each other honest, and those men—Dr. Lee Kliewer, Dr. Walter Ray, Dr. Charles Shields, and Dr. John Todd—have all read this manuscript and made good suggestions. Tom Edwards, David Leek, and Norman Lobsenz are professional writers as well as friends, so for them to go over this material took time from their own writing, and for that I am grateful. Kathy Hill knows cant when she sees it and has been indefatigable in her research. Dr. John Bulgian, Pat Henry, Ron Klug, Carol Lenters, Alan McGinnis, Jr., Inez McGinnis, Markus Svensson, Mike Somdal, and Dr. Robert Swinney were very helpful in their comments. Nancy Wagner has offered good marketing ideas, and my associate, Marilynn Surbeck, has been wonderful throughout.

On a rainy afternoon at Penn, Dr. Martin E. P. Seligmann responded to my questions as if he relished the chance to think aloud about the issues we were discussing, when in fact he had doubtless been asked the same questions a hundred times. Though he is the world's foremost authority on learned helplessness and certain aspects of optimism, he seemed quite unimpressed with his own importance that day and was generous with information and advice.

This is the fourth book on which Roland Seboldt and I have collaborated. Roland is the most cosmopolitan man I know in the publishing world. An inveterate traveler, he seems to know and love people in the book business everywhere. He is acute in his intuitions, honest in his opinions, considered in his recommendations, the soul of stability, a tireless advocate, an undiscourageable negotiator—in short, the kind of editor any writer would kill for.

Umberto Eco, the Italian semiotician and novelist, once recalled his early ambitions as a young man: "I [wanted] to make a book and a kid, because they are the only ways to overcome death, a paper thing and a flesh thing. Lovemaking alone, for all its pleasures, is stupid; nothing comes of it. But my death can have a sense if somebody survives me and continues. And I write a book, not to have a success now but with the hope that in the next millennium, it will be still at least in a bibliography or in a footnote." He is right: one's writing and one's children are curiously intertwined, and I wish to thank Sharon, Alan, Scott, and Donna for helping me believe that the best is yet to be.

Thanks also to my grandson Christopher, who is too young to read books like this, but who teaches me about the optimistic spirit every time he bounces into our house for a visit.

Finally, my appreciation to the patients who have allowed me to talk about them on these pages. When you are a therapist, your outlook is influenced by the people who tell you their stories. I find that mixed with the expressions of their pain, these people say some very wise things. They have *had* to learn wisdom, for some have grappled with problems so gargantuan that I marvel that they have survived them. The details of these patients' lives are of course scrambled here for purposes of confidentiality, but the shapes of their stories are, I hope, accurate.

Valley Counseling Center
Glendale, California

□ The Power
of *Optimism*

☐ Twelve Characteristics
of Tough-Minded Optimists

1 Optimists are seldom surprised by trouble.

2 Optimists look for partial solutions.

3 Optimists believe they have control over their future.

4 Optimists allow for regular renewal.

5 Optimists interrupt their negative trains of thought.

6 Optimists heighten their powers of appreciation.

7 Optimists use their imaginations to rehearse success.

8 Optimists are cheerful even when they can't be happy.

9 Optimists believe they have an almost unlimited capacity for stretching.

10 Optimists build lots of love into their lives.

11 Optimists like to swap good news.

12 Optimists accept what cannot be changed.

*The greatest discovery of my generation
is that human beings can alter their lives
by altering their attitudes of mind.*

WILLIAM JAMES

☐ How This Book Can Help You Become a More Optimistic Person

Have you ever wondered why some people are challenged by their problems and others are overwhelmed by them?

This is the sort of psychological puzzle we therapists ponder a great deal. What is it in some of our patients that enables them to bounce back, when others—with similar backgrounds, experiencing the same defeat—never recover? These tough-minded optimists may be of average intelligence and looks, but they know how to keep themselves motivated, and they approach their problems with a can-do philosophy. They are experts at building a strong, positive esprit de corps in their family or on their team, and they emerge from tragedies somehow stronger and more attractive.

There is no doubt that this mind-set enables people to rise to the top of their fields. Recent studies show that optimists excel in school, have better health, make more money, establish long and happy marriages, stay connected to their children, and perhaps even *live* longer.

1

A What-To-Do-Book

This book is written to delineate the intellectual habits of these successful people and to suggest ways you can put their habits to work in your own life. Before writing it, I plowed through all the psychological research I could find on what makes an optimist tick. However, I discovered there was more to learn by examining the lives of upbeat people. So I read almost a thousand biographies and analyzed the lives of many successful persons.

In studying these people I discovered a cluster of characteristics that most optimists have in common. These optimists were not necessarily born with cheerful dispositions, nor did they lead charmed lives. Far from it. Many grew up in very negative environments, and most suffered some crushing setbacks at one time or another. But along the way they discovered techniques for defeating depression and keeping their enthusiasm high. These psychological skills are so natural for some that they use them quite unconsciously. Others have had to turn themselves from pessimists into optimists through a deliberate plan of action. But the strategies they used to keep themselves motivated are remarkably similar, and the following chapters will explore in detail those strategies.

Can Pessimists Change?

In my work as a psychotherapist, I talk to many people who say they wish they *could* be more positive, but who think they are cursed with a pessimistic nature. Some say they have had a bleak attitude all their lives, and they are convinced they can never change. But when I explain that today's cognitive psychologists have developed practical, easy-to-follow steps for changing one's disposition, and that the habits of thought optimists employ can be learned by anyone, these people brighten up. For no one *wants* to be a pessimist.

Tough-Minded Optimists

On the other hand, most of us do not want to be Pollyanna, hear-no-evil-see-no-evil types either. So this book's approach is highly practical. I suggest realistic, workable ways to face difficulties squarely and at the same time keep an optimistic frame of mind.

Some of these ideas are as old as the Bible; others are newly minted from recent psychological research. But all are sensible strategies that have helped hundreds of our clients overcome discouragement and depression. I give examples to demonstrate how you can be less discouraged and depressed by circumstances, and how you can develop mental techniques that will give you a cheerful disposition, increased physical vigor, an aptitude for success, and rich, warm relationships.

These may seem extravagant claims, but they are based on true stories of real people who have learned to be happy in their daily lives and productive in their careers.

Self-Improvement

One of the best things about these principles is that most people do not need years of counseling to make them work. Many of the stories contained in the following pages are about pessimists who learned new attitudes and new approaches to problems entirely on their own, without any help from a mental-health professional such as myself.

It would be foolish to say that there is any one "secret" to leading a cheerful, high-energy life. Practical optimists use different tools to cope with different situations, and it is the totality of these qualities that makes them successful. But in the chapters that follow, I have distilled these qualities to twelve basic characteristics of optimists, with a chapter devoted to each characteristic. I believe that anyone who carefully studies these chapters can learn methods of daily living that will bring genuine happiness and contentment. Changing the way you think is never easy, but if you diligently devote yourself to mastering these characteristics, you reap enormous dividends.

Life is not the way it's supposed to be.
It's the way it is. The way you cope with
it is what makes the difference.

VIRGINIA SATIR

1 □ Pollyanna Won't Help Us Here

There is a soft-headed type of thinking that masquerades as optimism, but it is quite different from the practical approach that brings success. Some people who believe things are getting better feel foolish when things get worse. As a result, they often become disillusioned and cynical. But tough-minded optimists are aware that they live in an imperfect world in which love ends, innocent people are cheated, and sick people die.

Characteristic number one then is:

☐ *Optimists are seldom surprised by trouble.*

In February 1901, young Winston Churchill, slim and elegant at twenty-six, rose to make his inaugural speech in the House of Commons. This was to be his stage for the next fifty years, and on it he was to receive almost constant criticism and suffer many humiliating defeats. In those early years he was probably the most hated man in the House of Commons. The Blenheim Rat, his foes called him.

Thirty-eight years later, when Great Britain was on the verge of collapse from Hitler's assaults, King George VI asked Churchill to form a new government. By now he was sixty-five, the oldest head of state in Europe. The crusty politician had lived too long and was too battle-scarred to put on a false smile or to talk in Pollyanna terms about the future. "I have nothing to offer but blood, toil, tears, and sweat," he told his countrymen that Sunday night in May 1940. Yet laced with this blunt realism was a fierce relish for the coming combat, and a belief that the dispirited and ill-equipped British nation could control its destiny. After the fall of France, Churchill said, "We shall fight on the beaches, we shall fight on the landing grounds, . . . we shall fight in the hills; we shall never surrender."

It was this mixture of realism and determined hope that eventually won the day for the Allies. And it is this same mix that empowers every successful person.

How do we maintain such a balanced approach to trouble? Here are some strategies.

Strategy # 1: Think of yourself as a problem solver.

If there were one huge tranquilizer that would render us oblivious to all our problems, few of us would take it, because we know trouble often brings out the best in us. The finest salesman I know is Mike Somdal, who, before he went on to bigger things, was my literary agent. In those early years I was an unknown and unpublished writer, and when we made trips to see publishers we were not always welcomed with open arms.

One day we made what I thought was a superb proposal to an editor, but it was rejected on the spot. Walking back to our hotel, I was discouraged and despondent, almost ready to give up.

But not Mike. When we reached our room he began pacing the floor like a general, deep in thought. Suddenly he rubbed his hands together and exclaimed, "This is when selling gets fun. There's a way to go back and appeal to those people's needs, and when we do, they'll *beg* to buy from us. All we have to do is figure out the right approach!"

What I regarded as failure he shrugged off as merely the sort of setback everybody encounters when they dream big. His energies actually seemed to be recharged by this challenge. Within months a new approach was successful, and we negotiated contracts with some of the very publishers who had turned us away earlier.

Mike is a success at almost everything he attempts,

primarily because he thinks of himself as a problem solver, a troubleshooter, a person who excels in stressful situations. When he hits the wall, he simply pulls back and figures out another way over or around.

For their book *Leaders,* Warren Bennis and Burt Nanus interviewed many of the world's foremost managers. A striking characteristic distinguished them from the general population. "They simply don't think about failure," the authors observe. "They don't even use the word. They rely on synonyms such as 'mistake,' 'glitch,' 'bungle,' or countless others such as 'false start,' 'mess,' 'hash,' 'bollix,' 'setback,' and 'error.' Never *failure.*"

Strategy # 2: Look for multiple options.

Optimistic people are successes not only because they see themselves as problem solvers but also because their minds hold an arsenal of alternatives. When one approach fails, they simply move on to another option.

Homer's *Odyssey* has a wonderful scene in which Odysseus' son is worried that his father will never come home from the wars. But Pallas Athene, the heroine of the book, gently reassures him: "Your father will not be exiled much longer. . . . Trust Odysseus to get free, *he always finds a way.*" It is an apt description of the tough-minded optimists we're discussing: They always find a way. They keep trying, experimenting, looking. And eventually one of their experiments works. When Odysseus does get home in time to drive away his wife's suitors and reunite his family, it is perhaps the greatest homecoming scene in all of literature.

Let's take a more modern analogy. When one watches a skilled running back in football, what may appear to be a tuck-your-head-and-hit-the-line-hard-enough-to-get-through method is actually a lesson in the exercise of alternatives. The runner is making dozens of split-second adjustments and changes of direction as he runs, constantly looking for openings in what seems like an unbreachable line of opposition—in short, seeking alternate solutions.

Such adaptability is a characteristic of successful people in many fields. A young man by the name of James Whistler was a cadet at West Point with aspirations to become a career officer, but he couldn't pass chemistry and eventually was dismissed. Without looking back, he turned to painting and went on to become one of the most sought-after artists of his generation. Whistler said that if silicone had been a gas, he would have been a major general. But if he had become a major general, we would have been deprived of such famous paintings as *The White Girl* and *The Artist's Mother,* and some of the finest etchings in the world.

Julio Iglesias was a professional soccer player in Madrid when a car accident left him paralyzed for more than a year and destroyed his career. To help Iglesias pass the time in the hospital, a nurse gave him a guitar. Although Iglesias had no prior musical plans, he went on to become a pop music star.

In his pursuit of the incandescent light bulb, Thomas Edison tried experiment after experiment that failed. "Shucks," he told a discouraged co-worker during one trying series of experiments, "we haven't failed. We now know a thousand things that won't work, so we're that much closer to finding what will."

Strategy # 3: Anticipate problems.

Is it possible to be too positive? Of course it is. We all know people whose reckless optimism got them into trouble. They borrowed too heavily, they were overly optimistic about sales, they failed to anticipate delays, and consequently their businesses failed.

Tough-minded optimists, on the other hand, anticipate problems. In September 1960, an American drug company applied to the U.S. Food and Drug Administration for a license to dispense a new sleeping pill widely used in Europe as a sedative and for morning sickness in pregnant women. The pill gave prompt, deep, natural sleep without a hangover. It was cheap and produced no ill effects when tried on animals. There seemed to be every reason that the drug would be approved. But the application landed on the desk of Dr. Frances Kelsey, a mother of two teenage daughters. Dr. Kelsey had many questions about the drug. The fact that its effects on experimental animals were not the same as on human beings troubled her, and she asked for more studies.

The American manufacturer, sure it had good evidence for the drug's safety, had the medicine packaged and on pallets ready to ship. The company submitted a flow of reports and studies, keeping the pressure on. But Kelsey still had reservations and would not be hurried. Then on November 29, 1961, a cablegram from Europe informed them that the drug was causing an epidemic of birth defects, and the next day the application was withdrawn.

The drug—thalidomide—proved to be one of the most infamous pharmaceutical disasters of this century. Thousands of European children were born without arms and legs. There were also deformities of the eyes, esophagus, and intestinal tract. One out of three of these children died.

At a White House ceremony in August 1962, President Kennedy awarded Dr. Kelsey the President's Award for Distinguished Federal Civilian Service, the top honor for U.S. government workers. All because she anticipated problems.

A successful real estate developer in my city is both a cheerful person and an astute businessman. I once talked to him about the source of his high spirits. He said, "I always try to do two things:

- I always ask, 'What I can do to make a bad situation better?'
- I try to plan ahead to avoid bad situations whenever possible."

His second rule may be more important than the first. There are times when negative thinking will prevent future failures. Being optimistic does not require your saying yes to everyone who wants your time or your money. If you are making an investment, approving a color scheme, or interviewing a job applicant, you need to think of worst-case scenarios. The hard-headed optimist asks discriminating questions: "What potential problems exist here?" "How could this be improved?" "Is there a way this will backfire?" "Where could we get cheated in this deal?"

Optimists are aware that things can go wrong and that there are people who, if we let them, will take our jobs, our money, and even our mates. Sinclair Lewis once received a letter from a very young and very pretty woman who wished to become his secretary. She said she could type, file, and anything else, and concluded, "When I say anything, I mean *anything*." Lewis turned the letter over to his wife, Dorothy Thompson. She wrote to the young woman saying, "Mr. Lewis already has an excellent secretary who can type and file. I do everything else, and when I say everything, I mean *everything*."

That was not cynicism. It was enlightened self-interest which headed off problems before they developed.

Strategy # 4: Talk freely about negative feelings.

A woman with terminal cancer said to me, "I'm not afraid to die, but I can't stand what this is doing to my family. Is there something you could say to cheer up Jack?"

"Rita," I replied, "if I were to slap your husband on the back and say, 'Snap out of it, don't take it so hard,' that would be an insult. He doesn't *want* to be happy at a time like this. He loves you very much, and because he does, it's the most natural thing in the world for him to grieve. His sadness has something almost noble to it."

She thought awhile and said, "Maybe you're right. That helps."

Tears are often a gift from God, and sadness is a healthy emotion. One day in the spring of 1953, George and Barbara Bush were told that their three-year-old daughter, Robin, had leukemia. She hung on for eight months, with Barbara, whose hair began turning white, sitting at her bedside.

Friends say George and Barbara Bush "handed their grief back and forth, acting alternately as mourner and supporter." It is the ideal way for two people to process a tragic event. Mrs. Bush says, "George held me tight and wouldn't let me go. You know, [many] people who lose children get divorced because one doesn't talk to the other. He did not allow that."

Depression is often caused by swallowing some negative emotion, most commonly anger or grief. (Although sadness and depression look alike and are often confused, they actually are quite different. Depression is not so much a feeling of sadness as a reduction of feeling.) So the road to optimism is not the denial of such emotions. On the contrary, accepting and expressing them are sometimes the first steps out of depression. As some sage has said, "The way out is sometimes *through*."

Strategy #5: Look for the good in bad situations.

At age fifty-two, C. S. Lewis was a professor of literature at Magdalen College, Oxford; a world-famous Christian apologist; and a resolute bachelor, who, according to some accounts, was quite uncomfortable with women. Describing himself to a class of fifth graders who had written to him from Rockville, Maryland, he wrote: "I am tall, fat, rather bald, red-faced, double-chinned, black-haired, have a deep voice, and wear glasses for reading. Best love to you all. When you say your prayers, sometime ask God to bless me."

Then in 1952, Lewis met Joy Davidman, an American poet with two young sons. A former atheist and communist, she had been converted to Christianity, in part from reading Lewis's books. Those who knew Lewis were amazed that this erudite professor, who had always sought out male companionship, now began to spend so many evenings with the young, attractive American woman. The British Home Office would not renew Davidman's visa, so Lewis matter of factly proposed a civil marriage, merely as a formality, to make her a British citizen. Life could go on, he assured her, "separate households and all that." Annulment was hers whenever she wanted it. And so on April 23, 1956, with only two witnesses, Lewis and Davidman were married before a magistrate.

A curious thing now happened. Though the couple continued to live in separate households, they gradually fell in love. "It began in Agape, proceeded to Philia, then became pity, and only after that, Eros," Lewis wrote. At about the same time, Joy fell ill. Alone at home one night, she tripped over a telephone cord and passed out. At the hospital she was diagnosed with cancer.

Lewis considered them still unmarried because there had been no Christian wedding. So in Davidman's hospital room an Anglican priest conducted the religious ceremony. During the next three years, Joy had long reprieves from her illness. She moved, with her sons, into The Kilns, Lewis's home.

Though Lewis knew these reprieves must eventually end, he was inconsolable when, at last, his wife died. "No one ever told me that grief felt so like fear," he wrote in a notebook. "I am not afraid, but the sensation is like being afraid. The same fluttering in the stomach, the same restlessness, the yawning. . . . She was my daughter and my mother, my pupil and my teacher, my subject and my sovereign; and always, holding all these in solution, my trusty comrade, friend, shipmate, fellow soldier. My mistress; but at the same time all that any man friend (and I have good ones) has ever been to me. . . . If we had never fallen in love, we should have nonetheless been always together, and created a scandal."

Lewis was bitter that he and Joy had so little time together. "Is it rational to believe in a bad God?" he wrote. "Anyway, is a God so bad as all that? The cosmic sadist, the spiteful imbecile?" From a therapist's viewpoint, such anger is quite healthy—even anger that rages for a while at God, for he is quite capable of handling such emotions.

Time is, of course, a great healer. Eventually Lewis began to emerge from his grief and went on to collect his angry scribblings into one of his most powerful books, *A Grief Observed*. Not only has the book made an important contribution to Christian literature, but in the process of writing it, Lewis came to terms with his wife's death. He was able to discover a great deal of good in a bad situation.

Thomas Edison is another example of a robust personality who never caved in to disaster and who knew how to turn an adversity into an advantage. In December 1914, the great Edison laboratories in West Orange, New Jersey, were almost entirely destroyed by fire. In one night Edison lost two million dollars' worth of equipment and the record of much of his life's work.

Edison's son Charles ran frantically about trying to find his father. Finally he came upon him, standing near the fire, his face ruddy in the glow, his white hair blown by the winter winds. "My heart ached for him," Charles Edison said. "He was no longer young, and everything was being destroyed. He spotted me. 'Where's your mother?' he shouted. 'Find her. Bring her here. She'll never see anything like this again as long as she lives.'"

The next morning, walking about the charred embers of so many of his hopes and dreams, the sixty-seven-year-old Edison said, "There is great value in disaster. All our mistakes are burned up. Thank God we can start anew."

This gift for turning stumbling blocks into stepping-stones will stand a person in good stead in every type of endeavor, in every group of people. On a late airplane the night before Thanksgiving a jolly salesman in the seat next to me said he had been flying all day from upstate New York and had been stranded for the evening in Salt Lake City. Because of the delay, he would not arrive home in Bakersfield until 2 A.M. But was he irritable and tired like most of the travelers in our packed plane? No, he was happily teasing the two little children across the aisle, spreading good cheer to the people around us.

"What do you sell?" I asked.

"Oil drilling tools."

"That's a tough business to be in these days, isn't it?"

"No," he replied. "It couldn't be better. We just opened another branch office this year and it's doing great."

"But isn't the oil business in a terrible recession?" I asked.

"Yes, but we've decided not to participate," he said with a smile. He went on to explain their success. "The industry slump has worked to our advantage because all our competitors are down in the mouth and complaining that they have to cut prices and can't make any money. That negative attitude rubs off on the customers. We, on the other hand, are not cutting our prices at all. But we're giving the best service of anybody in the industry, we're enthusiastic about our products, and we're very upbeat. Customers like doing business with salespeople who have that attitude."

He smiled again, and said, "If this recession will just continue one more year, I'll make enough money to retire."

Strategy # 6: Avoid phony pep talks.

Successful people do not talk about how wonderful things are when, in fact, they're bad. Certain people try to smile in the face of difficulties and declare that if everyone will be patient, things will turn out fine. But things usually do *not* turn out fine in such cases, because small problems, when ignored, have a way of turning into bigger problems, and soon you have a crisis on your hands.

Channing Pollock, after seeing the famous play about Pollyanna, wrote, "After I had stood two acts of Pollyanna's gladness, I went out into the night looking for a chance to assault a blind beggar. If I had lost my legs and that dreadful child had told me I should be delighted, because now I could 'sit down all the time,' I'm afraid I should have made her sitting temporarily difficult."

The Pollyanna approach simply will not help people who are going through the valley of the shadow. When Rabbi Harold S. Kushner's son Aaron was four, he and his wife were told that he had progeria, "rapid aging," which meant that he would never grow much beyond three feet in height, would have no hair on his head or body, and would look like a little man while he was still a child. Ten years later their son died. Kushner says that though he had been a theologian for many years, now he began to wrestle personally with the philosophical question of why such things happen, and his conclusion from reading the book of Job was that life is not always fair. Writing later, he said with simple eloquence, "Pain does not last forever, nor is it unbearable." In such situations he recommends doing three important things:

1. Belong to people.
2. Accept pain as part of life.
3. Know that you have made a difference.

Such statements are in a different category from the puny platitudes of the Pollyanna optimists.

At sales meetings one often hears a standard motivational talk intended to pump up the troops. It runs something like this: "You are wonderful in every way, your mind is a powerhouse, and if you will believe strongly enough, you can do anything." We've all heard that sort of thing many times. From the story of *The Little Engine That Could* to the latest self-help books, we've been told that if we have enough faith we can move mountains.

There is enough truth in these pep talks to make them attractive, but it is easy for motivational speakers to get so carried away that they become absurd. For instance, Napoleon Hill, in his book *Think and Grow Rich*, says:

Whatever
The Mind of Man
can
conceive
and
Believe
it can
Achieve.

That is claptrap, and such overstatements give faith and hope a bad name. Many of our patients who must be confined to a locked psychiatric ward would subscribe to such nonsense, and it is their grandiosity which helped get them in trouble.

Sometimes we don't realize how confusing and condescending it can be to tell people that if they simply lift their chins and have the right attitude, life can be fine. One woman says she never recalled hating anyone except a man who, on her first cruise, was almost the only passenger aboard who wasn't seasick. "He was a kind man," she said, "but when he sat on the edge of my chaise and told me how he enjoyed the motion, and why I needn't feel ill if I didn't give in, I decided I could stand anything that would lay him on his berth for the rest of the trip."

A phony pep talk is usually the last thing a group needs. What it may need is a leader who says, "We've got a mess on our hands, but if we all roll up our sleeves, we can do something about it."

There are no hopeless situations in life; there are only men who have grown hopeless about them.

CLARE BOOTH LUCE

Nobody makes a greater mistake than he who does nothing because he could only do a little.

EDMUND BURKE

2 □ The Search for Solutions

As we examine the traits of optimists, a recurring theme begins to emerge: Optimists are people of action. When there is trouble, they do not stand idly by, wringing their hands. Instead they wade in and get to work on some part of the problem, even if a full solution is not yet apparent. So characteristic number two is:

□ *Optimists look for partial solutions.*

Henry Ford once said that any task, no matter how large, is manageable if you break it down into small enough pieces, and most optimists think like Henry Ford: They bracket their work into manageable segments. They say, "I don't know how we're going to lick this thing, but at least here's one thing we can do today."

A young single mother once consulted me because things had gone from bad to worse since her divorce. She was a small, slight person, and she moved as if she were carrying twenty years of fatigue. Her ex-husband was behind on the support payments, her job was a dead-end, the children were sometimes more than she could handle, and her future looked bleak.

"The only bright spot in my life," she reported, "is that I'm in love with a man at work. He's married, and says he'll never leave his wife, but our affair has gone on two years now, and it's better than nothing."

"You're probably not going to like this," I told her at the end of the hour, "but you ought to get out of that relationship. It's wrong morally, and it's wrong psychologically. For you to stay there and gradually lose your soul when you could have something better—that's self-destructive."

"That's easy for you to say," she bristled. "The chances for a single mother with two kids are not all that great. And how is it going to help to leave him? I'd just be lonelier."

When a patient must make a tough decision, it doesn't

always lead to a wonderful life, but in this case the story has a happy ending. It took six months of turmoil, during which the relationship was on-again, off-again, but eventually the woman acknowledged she was being used, and she made a clean break from her lover. To help assuage her loneliness, she enrolled in some night classes. That, in turn, led to a new job, and there she met the man who is now her husband, and they recently had a baby of their own.

"When you've had a marriage go sour," she said recently, "and been in some destructive relationships, you're so grateful to have one that works. I can't imagine being married to a better guy or having a happier family."

How did her good fortune come about? From a series of partial solutions. She did what was right, even though she couldn't see the immediate benefits, and that action led to a series of resolutions.

It is noteworthy that when people came to Jesus, he often asked them to take some specific action. "Go, wash," he said to a blind man. "Stretch out your hand," he said to a crippled man. "Take up your bed and go home," he commanded a paralyzed man. When we arise from our lethargy and take some action, the action enhances our confidence.

How Two Men Faced Disaster

The darkest days of author Thomas Carlyle's life began when his friend, philosopher John Stuart Mill, came into his study one morning and told him that the manuscript Carlyle had given him to read was used by the maid to start the fire that morning.

It was the only copy.

Carlyle alternated between rage and grief, then settled into deep despair. One day he looked out his window and saw bricklayers at work. "It came to me," he wrote later, "that as they lay brick on brick, so could I still lay word on word, sentence on sentence." He began to rewrite *The French Revolution.* The work endures to this day as a classic and as an example of the achievement possible when, faced with a daunting journey, we simply put one foot in front of the other. Benjamin Franklin, in his *Autobiography,* wrote, "Human felicity is produced not so much by great pieces of good fortune that seldom happen as by little advantages that occur every day."

A man I know says he learned a coping mechanism in college that has helped him throughout his life. The impoverished school had no scholarship funds, his tuition money was gone, and he was ready to pack up his books in the middle of the semester and return to his farm home. But the president of the college learned he was leaving and called him in. When the president heard the student's story, he said, "Son, I don't know how we're going to keep you here, but we don't want you to go, so let's leave the impossible up to God and get busy with the possible."

The financial problems were eventually resolved, but my friend says that the lesson he learned in the president's office that day was worth far more than the tuition money. He is now an executive who manages more than five thousand workers. "That simple sentence about leaving the impossible up to God and getting busy with the possible has helped me in lots of so-called impossible situations," he says.

A Way to Cut Your Problems in Half

Successful people know that beginning is half the doing. The philosopher Aristotle is reputed to have said that the first step is what counts; that first beginnings are hardest to make, and as small and inconspicuous as they are, potent in influence; but once they are made it is easy to add the rest.

And Goethe says:

What you can do, or dream you can, begin it,
Boldness has genius, power and magic in it.
Only engage, and then the mind grows heated—
Begin it, and the work will be completed!

At the psychiatric clinic where I work, we consider our patients' problems half solved before we meet them. The reason? They have usually been considering therapy for years, and now that they have called and made an appointment, it is clear that they have finally decided to get started solving their problems. Beginning is half the cure.

Freeing Yourself from Perfectionism

Optimists are able to mobilize themselves in the face of tough problems because they usually have overcome any tendency toward perfectionism. They are happy enough to proceed with a partial solution for the time being.

A large number of the depressed people with whom I work are plagued with a need to do everything exactly right, and as a result they do very little. They admit their relentless standards are stressful and even unreasonable, but they think their pursuit of perfection drives them to levels of excellence and productivity they could not otherwise attain.

In fact, just the opposite may be the case. Perfectionists usually accomplish less, because they squander so much time paralyzed by a fear of failure. They are unwilling to attempt anything difficult until they see how they can finish it without any mishaps.

A fascinating study by David Burns, M.D., of thirty-four successful, high-salaried salespeople showed that eighteen had perfectionistic ways of thinking while sixteen were nonperfectionistic. Burns anticipated that the highest salaries would be earned by the perfectionists. But the trend was in the opposite direction. Perfectionists who linked self-worth with achievement earned an average of $15,000 a year less than the nonperfectionists. They were actually paying a price in dollars for their mental strait-jacket.

Two Ancient Heroes

The Old Testament tells an arresting story about the power possessed by people who are not afraid to act. When the children of Israel were near the Promised Land, Moses sent twelve spies over the border for reconnaissance. When they returned after forty days, the majority report was two-fold: (1) The land is a wonderful place. It flows with milk and honey, and we have even brought back samples of the fruit that grows there. (2) Alas, we can never take the land because the cities are well fortified, and worst of all, there are giants there.

Two of the spies, Caleb and Joshua, made a minority report that was more hopeful. "Let us go up at once and occupy the land, for we are well able to overcome it," they said. These two were not looking at the situation through rose-colored glasses; they agreed that the giants were awe-some and that taking the cities would be difficult. "But the Lord is with us; do not fear them," they said.

What was the crowd's response? They sided with the pessimists. They wept and wailed all night and began to make plans to return to Egypt. One should never under-estimate the power of a few crepe hangers and doomsayers. They can sway a crowd very easily. Optimism and enthusi-asm are contagious, but they are not nearly so contagious as pessimism and doubt.

So Moses and his people languished for years there within sight of the Promised Land. The ten pessimistic spies perished in the desert of Sinai, their bones left to bleach on the plains of their doubts. And what happened to the two who were determined to act in faith? They eventually led the successful conquest of the Promised Land.

It would be interesting to know if Caleb and Joshua were 100 percent sure of success. I doubt that they were. Optimists are not crazy; they have no certainty they will succeed every time they take on tasks others will not touch. But they consider alternatives, they interpret data as optimistically as possible, and they cannot *stand* to quit if there is any prospect of success.

It is usually a small minority who dare to believe the impossible can be solved, who are willing to start scaling the mountain even though at the time they have no idea how they will conquer the summit. And it is usually just such people who end up on top.

How to Fail Successfully

Pragmatic optimists usually make the most efficient workers because they will try anything. Nancy Woodhull, a college dropout, made it from the newsroom to the boardroom by taking on new projects, regardless of the chances for failure. She was one of the start-up editors for *USA Today*, and now, at forty-four, she heads two major divisions of the Gannett Company, the media giant that owns, in addition to *USA Today*, eighty-three daily regional newspapers, sixteen radio stations, and ten television stations. Woodhull is the first to admit she has made some major missteps during her career. But people attribute her success to this very willingness to continue acting boldly after being bruised. "Nothing sits on Nancy's desk," says Mindi Keirnan, one of her top lieutenants. "It may not go in the direction you want, but it moves."

Optimists have an almost cavalier attitude toward failure. A successful woman I know was talking to one of her sons about jumping in and attempting more things. She wanted him to run for offices at school and participate in more activities. He replied, "Mom, you don't understand how hard it is for me, because you succeed at everything you do."

"I was amazed at his remark," she said, "because I fail more often than anybody I know. I may give a different impression simply because it doesn't bother me that much to fail, so I try more things than the average person. And given the law of averages, if you try enough things, you're going to succeed a lot."

The Rabbi on Baseball

A troubled man went to see a wise and good rabbi.

"Rabbi," he said, wringing his hands, "I am a failure. More than half the time I do not succeed in doing what I must do."

"Oh?" said the rabbi.

"Please say something wise, rabbi."

After much pondering the rabbi spoke as follows: "Ah, my son, I give you this wisdom: Go and look on page 930 of the *New York Times Almanac* for the year 1970, and you will find peace of mind maybe."

This is what he found: the listing of the lifetime batting averages of all the greatest baseball players. Ty Cobb, the greatest slugger of all, had a lifetime average of only .367.

The man went back to the rabbi and said, "Ty Cobb— .367. That's it?"

"That's it," said the rabbi. "Ty Cobb got a hit once out of every three times at bat. He didn't even bat .500, so what can *you* expect already?"

"Ah," said the man, who thought he was a wretched failure because he failed only half the time.

The Case of the Man Who Thought He Was Too Optimistic

Perhaps I can best illustrate the practicality of these ideas through the story of a man I met at a sales conference in Denver. In my speech that morning, I had tried to make some suggestions on how to combine an optimistic attitude with tough-minded realism—the basic material contained in this book. While greeting people on the platform, I noticed a distraught-looking man hanging back. When the others had left, he said rather defiantly, "Disagreed with almost everything you said this morning, Doc. My problem is that I've been too optimistic, and because I trusted people, now I'm getting royally shafted."

I asked if I could buy him lunch.

He ordered the first of several drinks and launched into a sad, angry tale. He had been a top-ranked salesman in his region until his wife had left him two years earlier. They had been in and out of court since, wrangling about support and custody of the children. Now his teenage daughter would not talk to him, and he was so depressed he could barely work.

"All I want to do is get this divorce over," he said. "Then I don't care what happens."

I tried to find something constructive to build on and asked about his customers. "You've been a good salesman. You must have some good friends among your clients?"

"No, they're only interested in what they can get out of me, like everybody else."

"What about your company, your manager?"

"They're being rats about all this, too," he said. "I'm

about to get canned, and to tell you the truth, I don't care if they do fire me. It would serve my wife right if I couldn't make the support payments."

I was beginning to suspect that this fellow had never been much of an optimist. In fact, he had one of the bleakest outlooks of anyone I'd ever met, but I was sure there must be a touch of hope somewhere in him.

"Do you still love your wife?" I asked.

"Yes, I do," he answered quickly.

"Are you sure she wants a divorce?"

"Well, she says she would come back if I'd stop drinking and get some counseling, but that's probably just a ploy to hurt me more. Besides, I don't believe in counseling. I don't even know why I'm talking to you."

I wasn't sure either, but it was clear his situation held more promise than he had been willing to admit at first. We talked for most of the afternoon about the variety of alternatives possible, how he was not as boxed in as it seemed, and how he could improve his attitude with simple, proven techniques. I told him that although no one could be sure that his marriage was salvageable, there were many small changes he could make. If he took enough small steps in the right direction, the cumulative effect could be startling. When we parted, he asked for the name of a marriage counselor in his city.

I have not seen that salesman in the ensuing years, but we talk by phone occasionally, and I look forward to getting his Christmas card each year because it always contains a new picture of his family. After some false starts, he and his wife were reunited. He now goes to Alcoholics Anonymous regularly, is active in his church, and last year was the highest-paid salesperson in his entire company.

*Nothing splendid has ever been achieved
except by those who dared believe
that something inside them was
superior to circumstance.*

BRUCE BARTON

3 □ Taking Charge
of Your Future

If we agree that practical optimists are people of action, it is useful to probe a little deeper into the sources of this spunk. Why do some people get moving, while others sit wringing their hands? What motivates some to chip away at a problem, even when the solution is not yet apparent? It is characteristic number three:

□ *Optimists believe they have control over their futures.*

The question of control turns out to be quite complex. Many people who come to a psychiatric clinic like ours are failing to get what they want because they drift along without clear goals. Or if they have goals, they lack a disciplined plan for reaching them. At first I saw these patients as lazy, so I tried a variety of motivational speeches to get them out and moving. But I soon discovered that my little sermons were having no effect. A glazed look would come over their eyes as I talked. The more eloquently I waxed about their infinite possibilities and the value of perseverance, the more disinterested they grew.

Looking back, I don't know why it took so long to discover that these patients had a distinct set of convictions about the way life works, and until I could help them change their belief system, no amount of inspirational talk was going to touch them. These patients were not lazy. They were pessimistic and passive *because they believed that they had no power to control their world.*

In trying to understand the origins of this resignation, I went back to read some famous research by psychologist Martin E. P. Seligman on what he called learned helplessness. His studies revealed that depressed people usually have had experiences from which they concluded that no matter how hard they try, there will always be opposing forces stronger than they are. Consequently, they become helpless and depressed.

Consider a patient with whom I worked for more than two years. When she was nine, her mother was killed in an auto accident. It is not hard to understand why she grew up with a hard crust around her. She not only feared that more disaster might strike at any time, but she also believed that whatever might happen to her was largely beyond her control. Her mother's accident may have been a fluke, but one such event can become the basis of a person's entire world view.

Conversely, the hard-headed believers we're discussing have acquired—sometimes also by a fluke—the belief that they have a great deal of power over their circumstances. This confidence that they are in the driver's seat helps them hold on long after others quit.

In spite of his paralysis from polio, Franklin D. Roosevelt possessed great physical stamina. When he returned to the capital after a whirlwind tour, appearing fresh and rested, he was asked how he could accomplish so much without being tired. Roosevelt answered, "You're looking at a man who spent two years trying to learn to wiggle his big toe."

Purveyors of Hope

Dr. Jerome D. Frank, the great Johns Hopkins psychiatrist, used to say that psychotherapists should above all be "purveyors of hope." Much of our job is to help people discover that in most situations their actions can affect the outcome, that what they do makes a difference.

An experiment in an Alabama hospital buttresses this point. E. S. Taulbee and H. W. Wright have created an "antidepression room" in which they seat depressed patients and then deliberately irritate them. They are, for instance, told to sand a block of wood, then reprimanded because they are sanding against the grain. After they switch to sanding with the grain, they are reprimanded for sanding with the grain. The abuse continues until the patients get angry. When they blow up, they are promptly led out of the room with apologies. Surprisingly often, the patients' depression begins to break up after this little exercise. When they discover that they can affect what happens to them, even in a minor way like getting a therapist off their back, the depression lifts.

The Power of the Small Success

Jungian analyst John Sanford tells about a depressed professional musician whom neither psychotherapy nor prayer was helping. One day the man's car had a flat on the highway. At first he stood there staring at the flat, realizing it had been years since he had changed a tire. Although he didn't know how to use the jack and tools in his car, he began to work at the task. After an hour of sweat and struggle, he finally got the spare tire on. Back in the car he realized he was no longer depressed!

What had happened is not all that complicated. The musician was faced with one more irritating problem. This time, rather than throwing up his hands and waiting for a mechanic, he took action and solved the difficulty himself. This small success showed him a way to approach his larger problems. He clearly had more control over his destiny than he thought.

How One Mother Inspired Her Son

General Electric is the tenth largest industrial corporation in the world. Its leader, Jack Welch, runs the company on the basis of a few tough but simple rules, such as:

- "Face reality as it is, not as it was or as you wish it were."
- "Change before you have to."
- "Control your own destiny, or someone else will."

The last belief is especially important. Where does someone as successful as Jack Welch get the conviction that he can control his destiny? "I was an only child," he says. "My parents were about forty when they had me, and they had been trying for sixteen years. My father was a railroad conductor, a good man, hardworking, passive. He went to work at 5:00 A.M., got home at 7:30 at night. My mother and I would drive down to the train station in Salem, Massachusetts, to pick him up. Often the train would be late, so we'd sit for hours and talk. I was very close to her. . . . She always felt I could do anything. It was my mother who trained me, taught me the facts of life. She wanted me to be independent. Control your own destiny—she always had that idea."

Bold and decisive leaders like Welch always assume they have power over their futures. On the other hand, there are people who blame all their troubles on circumstances: "Nobody could succeed with the boss I have" (". . . the husband I have," ". . . the financial problems I have"—the variations are endless). What they are actually saying is that the universe is stacked against them and they are powerless to change their world. Of course, if you believe you are impotent, you make yourself so.

Psychological Hardiness

When Thomas Edison was seven years old, a schoolteacher gave him up as a hopeless case. In the boy's presence, the teacher told an inspector that Edison was "addled" and that it was useless for him to attend school any longer. It is remarkable how frequently great men and women are misjudged in such a fashion before they become famous. I once saw on a college bulletin board a list of statements by teachers about their young charges that proved to be more than a little inaccurate:

Abraham Lincoln—"When you consider that Abe has had only four months of school, he is very good with his studies, but he is a daydreamer and asks foolish questions."

Woodrow Wilson—"Woodrow is a unique member of the class. He is ten years old and is only just beginning to read and write. He shows signs of improving, but you must not set your sights too high for him."

Albert Einstein—"Albert is a very poor student. He is mentally slow, unsociable, and is always daydreaming. He is spoiling it for the rest of the class. It would be in the best interests of all if he were removed from school at once."

Amelia Earhart, the pioneer aviator—"I am very concerned about Amelia. She is bright and full of curiosity, but her interest in bugs and other crawling things and her daredevil projects are just not fitting for a young lady. Perhaps we could channel her curiosity into a safe hobby."

Caruso's teacher told him that he had no voice. Admiral Byrd was retired from the Navy as "unfit for service." And an editor told Louisa May Alcott that she would "never be able to write anything for popular consumption."

Here is the interesting aspect of these biographies: Evidently each person came to realize early in life that authority figures were not the determiners of their destinies. Rather, they themselves were. They discovered that they could, with effort, overcome their adversities and prove such negative predictions to be wrong. That psychologically hardy attitude became their method for dealing with each future challenge.

The Virtue of Passion

What is the source of this extreme self-confidence found in almost all optimists, this conviction that they can accomplish great things? Do they have an exaggerated view of their abilities? Usually not. Many optimists I know are quick to point out that others have talents superior to theirs. Yet they are confident they can accomplish almost anything and have almost anything they want. The intangible quality that separates many successful people from talented people who fail is the sheer force of their wills. They have stronger passions, greater desires than average.

A young man who aspired to the study of law once wrote Lincoln for advice. Lincoln replied, "If you are resolutely determined to make a lawyer of yourself, the thing is more than half done already. Always bear in mind that your resolution to succeed is more important than any other thing."

A salesman said this about his beginnings:

When I began my career, I took stock of myself and added up my assets and liabilities. I was appalled at the extent of my liabilities. I had no sales experience, no extensive education, no voice training, and certainly no captivating personality. Apparently I lacked nearly all the attributes of the master salesman.

As far as assets were concerned, I could find only one. That was a determination so strong it amounted almost to an obsession—a burning, overwhelming desire to become a top salesman. Even at that early age I considered this quality an asset for the simple reason that I never heard of anyone achieving success who didn't want to achieve it.

If we knew nothing more about that man apart from this declaration, we could predict that he would go to the top.

40

□ *Optimists believe they have control over their futures.*

Perhaps not immediately, perhaps not in the first years of his career, but eventually he would succeed. In fact, he did just that and retired a very wealthy man.

Tommy Lasorda, manager of the Los Angeles Dodgers, is fond of saying to his team, "Races are not won by the fastest athletes. Fights are not won by the strongest men. But the races are won and the fights are won by those who want to win most of all." Desire and willpower are not the only ingredients for achievement, of course. There is such a thing as talent. Willpower may not override talent, but it continues to be the factor that causes people of ordinary ability to accomplish extraordinary things.

To sum up characteristic number three, optimists are people of action because they believe they have a great deal of control over the future. They are likely to carry with them a fervent desire for success, and they know that this passion can propel them for long distances when lesser people—people who sometimes have greater talent—will fall by the wayside.

It isn't the incompetent who destroy an organization. . . . It is those who have achieved something and want to rest upon their achievements.

CHARLES SORENSON

4 □ How to Increase Your Energy

When I had last seen him, he was at least forty pounds overweight, he was drinking and smoking too much, and his wife had finally left him in disgust. Though he had been a popular professor with many of us, he had become irresponsible—always late to lectures, sometimes never showing up at all. Eventually he was fired, apparently on a trajectory to oblivion.

When we ran into each other in a different city six years later, he was a different man. He had slimmed down, had a new wife and a new job. He was in a twelve-step program and had just published a book that was garnering excellent reviews.

What accounts for such a metamorphosis? Within us there seems to lie an instinct for self-healing, for restoration and renewal. Some do not grab for it on the way down, as my friend did. But that capacity for renaissance is in everyone, and it offers vast hope for the person who has run out of motivation.

Characteristic number four is:

□ *Optimists allow for regular renewal.*

In physics, the law of entropy says that all systems, left unattended, will run down. Unless new energy is pumped in, the organism will disintegrate. Entropy is at work in many areas other than physics. I see it, for instance, when I work with couples whose marriages are in trouble. A marriage will not continue to be good simply because two people love each other, are compatible, and get off to a fine start. To the contrary, marriages left to their own devices tend to wear out, break down, and ultimately disintegrate. This is the law of entropy. So to keep our relationships working, we must constantly pump new energy into them.

Entropy works within individuals as well. I see many patients who seem to have a good life, but then something happens. They find themselves losing interest in sex, getting bored with their work, growing discouraged about their futures. They come to therapy wondering if something is wrong with them. Often the problem is simply that they have not been doing enough to nurture themselves internally. They have assumed that their internal engine, unattended and unrefreshed, will go on indefinitely. But no machine works that way. Albert Schweitzer once wrote that some "harm their souls . . . without being exposed to great temptations. They simply let their souls wither. They allow themselves to be dulled by the joys and worries and distractions of life, not realizing that thoughts which earlier meant a great deal to them in their youth turned into meaningless sounds."

People who keep up their optimism and maintain their enthusiasm over the years are those who take measures, consciously or unconsciously, to counteract personal entropy, to make certain that the system does not quit on them.

Here are some suggestions for tapping the sources of energy within you and maintaining enthusiasm year after year.

Strategy # 1. Attach yourself to hopeful people.

Optimists do not spend much time fraternizing with negative people. They know that to keep their batteries charged, they must associate with enthusiastic individuals. This is not to say you should drop all your unhappy friends and associate only with successful people. Dr. Sam Shoemaker, the founder of Faith at Work, used to say you should take on two or three neurotics as your project—that is, people to whom you always expect to give more than you receive. "But don't take on too many," he advised, "because they can drown you."

We have a great deal of discretion over our associates. We know certain friends and family members pick us up and make us feel our power, whereas others pull us down and get us in the habit of thinking negatively. Optimistic people, when given a choice, spend time with those who pick them up. They take advantage of the electricity that can be generated when two or three people of hope are together.

Strategy # 2: Change your intellectual habits.

I know a businessman who decided to master Homer's great epic poem, the *Iliad*. He says he has read it six times during the past two years. "Though I certainly haven't mastered the thing," he says, "I'm beginning to see why it's such a classic. It is now a part of me, and I think I'm better for it." Reading something totally different can be such a stimulant. Perhaps you need to change your magazine subscriptions and get a fresh stimulus from new sources.

A couple who thought their evenings were getting dull agreed to turn off the television every night for an hour and spend the time reading aloud. "No magazines, no romance novels, and no books related to his business or mine," she says. "We read some philosophy and some theology, and really got into Churchill's history of World War II. Will I ever use this stuff in my business? I doubt it. But we found that after doing this every evening for a few weeks, our powers of concentration increased, and now we have dozens of books on our list to go through. Many evenings we never turn on the stupid television."

I occasionally give seminars for IBM, which requires its executives and sales personnel to get a minimum of forty hours per year of continuing education on company time. For a company IBM's size, that is an enormous investment, but it is an investment that pays, because knowledge is power. Disraeli once said that all other things being equal, the person who succeeds will be the person with the best information. When we think about the people we've known who have seemed happiest and most alive, are they not the ones who have been constantly expanding their interests and knowledge, who continued to have a thirst for learning? Education is a lifelong affair.

Strategy # 3: Feed your spiritual side with care.

In our graduate school the students sometimes laughed at Emile Cailliet, a French mystic and professor of philosophy. He was eccentric enough to arouse laughter, all right. He appeared to have only one suit—black. His shirt collars were usually askew, pointing sideways or upwards. He stared out the window as he lectured. But I found him the most stimulating teacher on campus. He couldn't remember the names of his students, but he could tell you on what page of what book a quotation was to be found, and his lectures were pure gold.

The term *burnout* had not yet acquired its present place in the language, but the phenomenon was of course prevalent. Such a state was caused, Cailliet told us, not by external pressure but by internal deterioration—what he called "a leakage of spiritual power." The phrase is apt. We all know people who started their careers with high ideals and zestful enthusiasm, but whose inner momentum gradually ran down—an entropic leakage of spiritual power.

Those who are able to stay energetic and enthusiastic over the long haul tend to have strong religious beliefs. Not all go to church, but I've noticed that there are few atheists among the go-getters, the crack salespeople, the hopeful people of this world. So if you find that your energy has evaporated and that you've lost some of your zest for the future, it may be that your spirituality needs a new commitment, that you must carve out time for reading and thinking about your faith, and above all, for prayer.

In his brutally honest diary, *The Road to Daybreak*, Henri J. M. Nouwen tells of his year in Trosly, France, working with L'Arche, the community formed to care for adults with severe mental handicaps. It was named after Noah's ark as a reminder that it would be a place where vulnerable men and women who are threatened by the judgmental and violent world in which they live could find a safe place and could feel at home. As Nouwen describes the exhausting regimen of the assistants who care for the residents, one wonders at their ability to remain sane themselves. Many of the residents are unable to walk, feed themselves, or even speak, and the assistants' days and nights are filled with cooking for them, feeding them, washing them, holding them during seizures. The assistants live in poverty and cannot escape the daily pain of their charges. How do such people keep going year after year? Here is Nouwen's telling comment: "Being at L'Arche means many things, but one of them is a call to a greater purity of heart." He goes on to describe the centrality in that community of L'Oratoire, the prayer room. It is a large space with small kneelers and little mats. Beautiful fresh flowers are always present, and on both sides of the wall people come and go throughout the day to kneel, sit, or lie down in prayer. (The handicapped people come as often as the assistants.)

Men and women have been renewing themselves by such means for thousands of years, and we can learn something from them which will help us in our modern households and businesses.

Strategy # 4: Talk to a young child.

Wordsworth said that children come into this world "trailing clouds of glory," and it is virtually impossible to stay depressed for long if there are little children in the room.

After a friend's funeral, we were asked to join the family

back at the house for lunch. I dreaded going, because we were all shocked and numb (he had died of a heart attack at fifty-six), and I worried about what I could say that would be of any help. When we walked in the door, I stopped worrying, because we heard the sound of little children's laughter. The widow was still crying some, but one of her grandsons was on her hip as she greeted the crowd, and he kept her laughing through her tears. All of us there seemed intuitively to grasp the lesson of that scene: that the planet continues to renew itself, that death is always counterbalanced by birth, and that when there are new young lives to be nurtured, we must go on. Jesus seemed to cherish children with an extraordinary appreciation for what they have to give us. Over and over in his teaching he made it clear that if we wish to know God, we must receive children and become like them.

One of the travesties of our culture is that retirement communities exist where families with children are actually forbidden to live. Everyone needs to be able to look out the window and watch some boys and girls playing on the sidewalk—senior citizens most of all. And every adult needs to get down on the floor and talk to some child eye-to-eye as often as possible. They are living containers of energy and excitement and love, and those attitudes spill over on us when we choose their companionship.

The Vietnamese monk, Thich Nhat Hanh, tells about sitting with a group of children. A boy named Tim was smiling beautifully.

I said, "Tim, you have a very beautiful smile."

And he said, "Thank you."

I told him, "You don't have to thank me; I have to thank you. Because of your smile, you make life more beautiful. Instead of saying "Thank you," you should say, "You're welcome."

Such an openness to the gifts of children will inevitably lead to renewal of the spirit. Hanh writes with profound simplicity: "Children understand very well that in each woman, in each man, there is a capacity of waking up, of understanding, and of loving. Many children have told me that they cannot show me anyone who does not have this capacity. Some people allow it to develop, and some do not, but everyone has it."

Strategy # 5: Make use of the ancient idea of the Sabbath.

It was not by accident that in Israel one day in seven was set apart for worship and rest. We need such openings to provide variety in our rhythm.

Tilden Edwards says that the question is not whether we move between action and rest, but how we do this. He argues persuasively for periods when we become receptive to what he calls "the graced quality of all life":

> My family tries to assure a Sabbath quality of time that, at its fullest, begins with dinner on Saturday evening and concludes with sundown on Sunday. We have evolved welcoming and closing rituals influenced by the Jewish Sabbath that mark off the time as "different." We try to keep work and worry to a minimum during that time, and appreciation of life as it is in God to a maximum. This is cultivated through especially good meals, candles, play, music, scripture, worship, quiet times, stories of hope, and anything else that seems helpful in setting off the period as especially receptive to life's giftedness.

Another family I know not only goes to church together on Sunday mornings, but they also make Sunday night a ritual. The grown children and their families, grandchildren, assorted boyfriends and girlfriends, all come back to the family home for a spaghetti dinner that evening. If someone has had a birthday during the week, it is cause for a big celebration. If two birthdays fall in the same week, they're never celebrated on the same Sunday. "Everyone should have one special day," the matriarch of the group says. Such rituals are the mortar that helps hold families together when crises come.

Sabbaticals, too, are sometimes necessary for renewal in business. John Sculley has been a remarkably successful businessman. After he became CEO of Apple Computers, revenues quadrupled to over $4 billion, and the return on shareholders' equity grew to be the highest in the computer industry. How does such a man stay fresh? One year Sculley took nine weeks off. He did not call it a vacation but a sabbatical. He and his wife went to Maine, where he designed a barn and took a course in photography. When he returned to work, he reported in *Fortune* magazine, he was filled with new ideas and was much better able to lead.

Some time ago I found myself writing too many articles, giving too many speeches, seeing too many patients, and not doing any of it well. So rather precipitously I went on leave. I stopped seeing patients and going to meetings. Instead, I took walks, laid bricks, planted trees, built some cabinets, changed the oil in our family cars myself for the first time in years, and spent more time with my grandson. I reexamined some of the mottoes I've always lived by, such as "We all produce better under pressure." If that motto was ever true (and I'm not sure it was), it didn't hold up under scrutiny for this stage of my life.

I read the Psalm, memorized some poetry, did lots of journal writing, spoke some Spanish, bought some new woodworking tools, mastered a new computer program, took naps every day, ate fresh foods, and hiked in the Sierras.

The result? After a few months my cholesterol was down a hundred points, and my blood pressure was reduced thirty points. I felt good physically for the first time in years. The family seemed closer. When I returned to church, I heard things I hadn't heard in years. And when I began to see patients again, the film was off my eyes.

Of course, it may be easier for psychotherapists like myself or company presidents like John Sculley to take time off from work, but you may have more options than you think. Most of us are not nearly so trapped by responsibilities as it seems. For instance, you can take short sabbaticals—two or three days in which you entirely alter your routine. Perhaps you can't control your job, but you may be able to change radically other things in your life to invite renewal. I live only three miles from my office, and found walking there to be a surprising stimulant. And on an all-day Saturday walk through the city of Los Angeles, I spent time meandering through the Mexican barrios, purposely staying off the main thoroughfares. Those good people's homes, their laughing children, and the strong family lives evident on a Saturday afternoon are still etched in my mind.

That brings us to the next suggestion:

Strategy # 6: Get to know someone new.

Get acquainted with new people, the more outside your regular orbit the better. Talk to everybody, and find someone new to love. I'm not advocating that you have an affair or switch mates, but that you find a neighbor or a colleague with whom you can make a good connection and who also might benefit from a new friendship. If it's someone much younger or much older than you, that's even better.

You might be awakened by getting to know someone from another culture. Not long ago, a boy came into our family's life who did wonders to rejuvenate us. For some bricklaying, I needed a day laborer to help, and that was the way I met José Percastegue. He was eighteen, had recently arrived from Mexico, and was hoping to make some money to send back to his family of twelve. Every day he wore the same pair of clean jeans with a broken zipper. Only after he had worked for us several days did we learn that he had no home and was sleeping in the alley behind the Methodist church. That night he moved in with us and has lived with us for more than two years now. In that time he has been a wonderful teacher.

We learned, for instance, that the joy of laughter has nothing to do with wealth or poverty. My wife was washing his clothes one day and one of his socks was missing. "Yes, sometimes our washer eats a sock," she said, as she pulled clothes out of the dryer. "Does that happen to your mother?"

"Sí," he replied with a laugh. "My mother washes in the river and sometimes the river eats a sock."

It may be surprising how fresh a perspective you can gain on your life and your relationships simply by pulling away and living in a different mode for awhile. So if you want to remain optimistic, look for ways to renew yourself, to open yourself for refreshment and revitalization. See different people, eat in different restaurants, change newspapers, take on fewer projects and do them better, discard some of your outdated mottoes, stay up late some nights, get up before dawn some days. Do anything to put an egg beater in your mind and stir things up.

Life does not consist mainly—or even
largely—of facts and happenings.
It consists mainly of the storm
of thoughts that are forever blowing
through one's mind.

MARK TWAIN

5 □ How to Change Your Patterns of Thought

A young midwestern lawyer had a dark side to his nature in his early years. On one occasion his friends thought it wise to keep knives and razors out of his reach and to have someone stay with him through the night. During this period he wrote, "I am now the most miserable man living. If what I feel were equally distributed to the whole human family, there would not be one cheerful face on earth. Whether I shall ever be better I cannot tell; I awfully forebode I shall not. To remain as I am is impossible; I must die or be better, it appears to me."

Those words were written in 1841 by Abraham Lincoln. His law partner, William Hearndon, said that "melancholy dripped from him as he walked" during that period. But note how different he sounds in 1863: "The year that is drawing toward the close," President Lincoln wrote, "has been filled with the blessings of fruitful fields and healthful skies. These bounties are so constantly enjoyed that we are prone to forget the source from which they come." He was painfully aware that thousands of America's young men were dying in the Civil War and that the country could be on the brink of collapse, but he was still able to see the goodness around him.

Sometime between 1841 and 1863, Lincoln had evidently learned certain habits of mind that enabled him to put much of his despairing tendencies behind him. Not that he became carefree and blithely happy in those years when the Republic shuddered; he would have been less a man had he suffered less. But he acquired an ability to live in the midst of tragedy and still cultivate qualities like gratitude and joy. A clue to Lincoln's character may lie in a casual remark he once made to someone on the subject. "I've noticed," he said, "that most people are about as happy as they make up their minds to be."

Lincoln probably would have liked the cognitive therapists who have been quietly revolutionizing the field of psychotherapy. For they are saying much the same thing. They contend that being a pessimist or an optimist is in large part a conscious decision, that we have considerable control over our moods, and—perhaps most important— that we can change the way we feel by correcting the way we think. The word *cognition* simply means thought or perception, and cognitive therapy is based on the simple idea that your thoughts, and not external events, create your moods.

This technique for modifying one's thought patterns is employed by all optimists, although most of them doubtless never heard of the cognitive therapists. It is characteristic number five:

☐ *Optimists interrupt their negative trains of thought.*

According to the cognitive therapists, it is a mistake to assume that emotions arise directly from events. Rather, they arise from the thoughts that events prompted. Here is an illustration: You see a car headed toward you. Label that event as *A*. Then you feel panic. But that emotion is *C*. Between the event and the emotion is *B*, the thought "He's going to hit me!" flashing through your mind. This sequence seems simple enough, but an understanding of it can have profound psychological ramifications for people who want to live optimistically. If it is our thoughts that cause us so many problems, then we therapists should stop asking our patients "How does that make you feel?" so frequently, and start asking "What are the thoughts that make you feel this way?"

Here are the steps for correcting your erroneous thought processes.

Strategy # 1: Monitor your automatic thoughts.

Because it is flowing through our minds so constantly and rapidly, we are largely unaware of the inner dialogue we carry on with ourselves every waking hour. Dr. Donald H. Meichenbaum, a brilliant psychologist at the University of Waterloo, Ontario, has used the label *automatic thoughts* for this subscript of inner appraisals, attributions, expectations, and self-questioning—all the material on which Woody Allen makes a living. It is an apt term. When we begin to slow down these thoughts and make them less automatic, the results can be quite illuminating.

Consider the case of a retired teacher who came to our clinic. She was quite depressed and because of the danger of suicide, she was immediately placed on antidepressant medication. In two weeks she was feeling better, so we began to work on correcting the way she thought about herself. I asked her to keep a log of all the negative ideas that ran through her head each day. "Oh, I don't think that'll be of much use," she said. "I've always been a very positive thinker."

However, when she came back for the next session she said, "I'm embarrassed for you to see how many pages I've written. I wouldn't have imagined that I thought so many dark, self-critical things. And now that I look at it, I realize these are ideas that have been running through my head for years." It was not a surprise, then, that these thoughts finally brought her down.

David Burns, M.D., works at the University of Pennsylvania, where much of the groundwork has been laid for cognitive therapy. He asks his patients to purchase the type of wrist counter used by golfers for keeping score. These patients wear the counter all day, punching it each time they catch themselves thinking a negative idea. At the end of each day, they write down the total score in a log book.

Burns reports that at first the number of critical thoughts increases as the person gets better at identifying them. Soon the daily total reaches a plateau for a week or ten days, then it begins to go down, indicating that the person is getting better.

Strategy # 2: Question whether your automatic thoughts are actually yours.

Once they begin monitoring their inner dialogue and learn to listen to this material playing in their minds, people realize that some of the thoughts are not really their own. Rather, they are quotations from other people that they have been collecting for years.

Let's say you are three years old and you are in the garage with your father, who is working on the car. His wrench slips, he skins his knuckles, and as his head emerges from under the hood, he swears, throws the wrench down, and says, "I'm so stupid, I can't do anything right." Or let's say you are a teenager working for a businessman who is always down in the mouth. At least every other day he says, "Business is okay now, but it'll probably be terrible next month." If you've grown up hearing such statements from people you admire, it is likely that twenty years later you'll find yourself saying "I'm so stupid" and throwing your wrench down when you're working on your car, or expecting that when business is good, it will turn sour.

Let me give another example from my counseling practice. A man sat slumped in my chair as he told about his recurring depression. I asked about his marriage.

"It's been hard," he said. "It's a wonder we're still together."

I asked about his career.

"That's been a struggle, too. Nothing has ever come easy for me."

As I pursued the details of his life, it was a recurring theme: *Everything* was hard. It didn't take a brilliant therapist to suspect that he had been programmed to view the world that way. Sure enough, it turned out that his parents had been gloomy, cynical people who would come home each evening to talk about how hard they had worked and how their day had been fraught with troubles. They conveyed to their children the notion that life was going to be a struggle, and they'd better be braced for lots of disappointments. So each time my patient undertook a new task, he said to himself, "This will be hard." And it usually was.

When we hear such ideas often enough, they become like tapes that automatically go on when certain situations activate them. Happily, once we recognize that these are quotations we've collected but do not necessarily believe, we can begin to revise them. Karl Menninger once said, "Fears are learned, and if they are learned, then they can be unlearned."

In this instance it took months of dogged therapy, during which we scrutinized his expectations one by one. Gradually he realized that he didn't concur with his parents' view of the world. He agreed that life is a mixture of good and bad, the tough and the easy, and he ventured that perhaps he could expect *some* things to go smoothly, to fall into place, to be easy. When he began repeating such beliefs to himself, his circumstances began to change dramatically. Tim Hansel, in his book *You Gotta Keep Dancin'*, says, "Pain is inevitable, but misery is optional."

Strategy # 3: Correct your cognitive distortions.

We've said that the first two steps in modifying your thoughts are to learn to listen to them and then to question negative ideas, asking whether they are echoes of someone else's voice or actually your own.

The third step is to question the logic of your automatic

thinking. Look for what the cognitive therapists call cognitive distortions.

In the process of questioning our logic, it helps to have labels for the cognitive distortions. Here are some basic labels.

Catastrophizing

You can make yourself miserable by repeating to yourself statements such as "I'll never get out of this mess. I can't stand all this stress. This has to be the worst day of my life."

This is "catastrophizing" the situation, and when we catch ourselves at it we should yell (though silently to ourselves) "Stop!" and make an on-the-spot modification. For instance, we can say to ourselves: "Now wait a minute, is it really true that I'll never get out of this mess? No, of course not. That was an overreaction. I *do* have a big problem here, and there's a lot of pressure, but I'll eventually get it solved. And can I stand this any longer? Sure, for a while at least, if I have to. Is this the worst day of my life? Hardly."

Selecting the Negative

Many of my clients have an interesting internal screen that seems to keep out positives but lets in negatives. When someone compliments them, they discount the compliment as a perfunctory courtesy and erase it from their memories quickly. But if they are criticized, the memory of that hurt lingers. They replay the criticism in their minds and can still recall it word for word years later.

Some minds are so constructed that they can only find the negative interesting. They note all the deaths and rapes and swindles and what is wrong with the world, while ignoring beauty, good fortune, and multiple illustrations of love and laughter around them.

Dr. Bruce Larson, who is a happy soul if there ever was one, tells about trying to spread some good cheer to a melancholy cabdriver who picked him up at the Indianapolis airport.

"It's a gorgeous day out here in Indiana," Larson said.

"You should have been here yesterday," said the cabbie. "It was terrible."

"You know, the autumn leaves are gone in Maryland, where I live, but your trees are still beautiful. I'm glad I came this week."

"These leaves will be gone in three or four days."

The fellow was so resolute in his gloom that by this time he had become a challenge. Larson looked out as they passed the Indianapolis Speedway and asked, "Isn't this the Indianapolis Speedway?"

"Yep."

"I'd sure like to see the race here some Memorial Day."

"I wouldn't go near it."

"Why not?"

"I'd rather watch the horses run."

At last my friend thought he'd discovered something the man liked. "Ah, you go to the track, then?"

"Nope, I never go. Too expensive."

How is it that many of us, like the cabdriver, get into such negative patterns? Largely by habit. Pessimism and hopelessness become almost a knee-jerk reaction. Our melancholy reactions, like twitches, become so instinctual that we do not realize how blind we have become to the good around us.

Generalizing

There is a logical fallacy we studied in freshman philosophy but of which we are guilty frequently: from one incident we jump to all sorts of wild generalizations.

Martin E. P. Seligman has designed a twenty-minute test to determine whether a person is an optimist or a pessimist. In assessing the person's attitude, Seligman looks for what he calls explanatory style. We all have certain habitual ways of explaining the bad things that happen, and it is the style of these explanations, Seligman says, that gives subtle clues to personality.

Seligman's questions are not complicated. He asks people if they see the causes of bad events as temporary or permanent, specific or all-encompassing. Some people place the worst possible interpretation on a failure. Let's say a young woman flunks a college test. If she explains it as being permanent ("I always mess up on tests"), all-encompassing ("I had just as well give up, because this is the way it'll be in all my classes"), we have a pessimist on our hands. On the other hand, says Seligman, certain people, when they fail, refuse to see it as permanent ("I failed that one, but it's not my pattern; I'll do better next time"). These optimists do not assume that if they're having trouble in one class, they'll have the same difficulty in every course. They tend to question the circumstances ("Who knows? Maybe it was a bad test and everybody had trouble"). Moreover, optimists usually see the setback as due to mistakes that can be remedied. If they are turned down for a job, they do not see it as a personal deficit that will plague them forever. Instead they ask other people for help and advice, then formulate a plan of action.

Personalizing

When Seligman is trying to smoke out pessimists with his test, he has one more question he asks: Do you blame yourself or someone else for failures? If you always say, "It must have been my fault," you have succumbed to the personalizing fallacy. For instance, when a teacher says your child is doing poorly in school, and the thought that instantly jumps up on the inner screen is "I must be a terrible mother," you are taking too much responsibility for failure. If an account goes to a competitor, and you automatically think, "I must be losing my touch," the same process is at work.

Dr. Albert Ellis, an early advocate of cognitive therapy, says that we walk around with about three to five hundred distorted ideas about ourselves. While the basis for his setting his numbers may be a little obscure, he makes a valid point. Some of us do mislabel ourselves several times a day. A patient with whom I was working drove to the market and absentmindedly turned on the wrong street. He found himself saying "What a dummy! I can't seem to do anything right today. It's going to take all afternoon to run these errands. Besides, I hate shopping."

The following week in my office he reported, "But then I interrupted myself and said, 'Okay, Norm, McGinnis tells me I can change my thoughts. Let's see what I can do with this.' So I tried to take those statements apart: 'Am I a dummy because I took the wrong turn? No, of course not. That's an illustration of mislabeling myself. I was just thinking about something else and missed a turn, that's all. I'll pull into this driveway, turn around, and be back on my way. Is it true that I can't do anything right? No, I make mistakes, but I do a lot of things right, so that's erroneous. And is this terrible? No, I was catastrophizing there. It's hardly a big disaster; I'm already back at the corner and probably didn't lose twenty seconds.' And you know, it was amazing how much more relaxed I felt when I stopped kicking myself all over the interior of my brain."

It should be noted that these correctives for our cognitive distortions are realistic and down-to-earth, quite unlike the extravagant self-talk advocated by some pop psychologists, especially the hot-tub variety we grow here in California. I once attended a lecture at which a grown man told us we ought to stand before the mirror naked every morning and repeat, "I love myself, I love myself, I love myself." That is ludicrous. Even some so-called affirmations, such as "I am a terrific person, this is going to be a marvelous day, and I will enjoy every moment of it," seem contrived and more euphoric than the facts warrant. The cognitive approach does not go overboard; it simply looks for instances in which our self-talk is unnecessarily bleak and can be recast more accurately.

I am now going to suggest an aid for interrupting and recasting your negative thought patterns. It is so simple that at first I refused to suggest it to my patients because I thought they would laugh. But Robert Oyler, a psychologist whom I respect, told me how effective it was, so I finally tried it on myself for a month and was converted.

The technique is this: You put a rubber band on your wrist and wear it twenty-four hours a day. When you catch yourself repeating one of your automatic negative thoughts, snap the rubber band. A few weeks of that can make you very aware of how often you repeat certain cognitive distortions.

Oyler buys rubber bands by the box and has been handing them out to his patients for years. "It seems like such a little thing," he says. "But I'll do anything to help a person interrupt depressive thoughts and replace them with something better. One of my patients made a remarkable turnaround in therapy, and her marriage was so improved that her husband was ecstatic. For their anniversary he said, 'Honey, this has been a great year emotionally and financially, and this is going to be our best anniversary. I'd like to buy you anything you'd like.' She thought a moment and said, 'That little rubber band was so important in turning my thinking around. Do you suppose we could have a jeweler make a gold bracelet in the form of a rubber band?'"

She wears it to this day.

Strategy # 4: Strive for favorable connotations.

Optimists not only interrupt their negative flow of thought and replace it with more logical assessments, they also try to see things in as favorable a light as possible. As a boy, Harry Bullis was thin as a rope, shy, and retiring. One day he took his dog out into the woods, sat on a stump, and made a crucial choice: "I decided to put the best possible connotation on the words and actions of every person and every situation. Naturally, I was not blind to the realities, but I always tried first to emphasize the best connotation, for I believe that such practice actually helps stimulate the outcome."

Bullis went on to become a powerful flour merchant in Minneapolis and an influential business leader throughout the Midwest. He was successful in part because he had trained his mind to interrupt negative thoughts and replace them with statements that viewed events in the best possible light.

We are what we think. This is one of the great universal truths, handed down by the poets and philosophers and by almost every religious leader. Bullis understood that truth and used it to his advantage.

To summarize the suggestions in this chapter:

1. Learn to monitor your automatic thoughts by listening to the stream of inner messages that precede your emotions.
2. Ask if some of these inner thoughts are genuine convictions or merely other people's ideas that have become embedded in your brain.
3. Learn to analyze your cognitive distortions by

category (catastrophizing, selecting the negative, generalizing, personalizing) and to make realistic corrections.

4. In making corrections, follow Harry Bullis's rule: Put the best possible connotation on the words and actions of every person and every situation.

*The person who has stopped being
thankful has fallen asleep in life.*

ROBERT LOUIS STEVENSON

6 □ The Selective Power of the Mind

Shortly after the Vietnam War, a friend drove up to a gas station in Arizona during a violent rainstorm. The attendant came out, whistling happily as he filled the gasoline tank. As my friend paid for the gas, he apologized for bringing the attendant out in such a downpour.

"That's all right," the attendant answered, his clothes dripping water into a puddle. "When I was lying in a foxhole in Vietnam, I vowed that if I got home alive, I'd be so grateful I wouldn't complain about anything again, and I haven't."

That young man's penchant for cheerfulness illustrates a general principle of living: Almost no situation is entirely good or entirely bad. But within us we possess an apparatus for selecting what we concentrate our attention upon, and we can direct that selective apparatus either way.

So characteristic number six is this:

□ *Optimists heighten their powers of appreciation.*

Said a sympathetic friend to a crippled woman, "Affliction does so color life."

"Yes," she replied, "but I propose to choose the color."

One of the tenets of this book is that we largely choose our attitude. We choose how to color our days and the events that occur in those days. Such a selection process goes on in the mind constantly. We can't possibly take in all the sights and sounds available to us at any given moment, so we select what we will see, what we will dwell upon.

St. Paul had this advice: "Whatever is true, whatever is honorable, whatever is just, whatever is pure, whatever is lovely, whatever is gracious, if there is any excellence, if there is anything worthy of praise, think about these things."

Behind this exhortation is Paul's assumption that we can choose the topics of our contemplation. This may be a rather strange idea in some psychological circles, where it is assumed that about all you can do is go with the flow and feel your feelings. But Paul asserts that the content of our minds is largely at our discretion and that by the use of this selective power we can alter our world.

Norman Vincent Peale tells of crossing the Hudson River on a pea-soup morning. The ferry was crowded with commuters grousing and complaining about the weather. His elderly mother was with him, and as she stood at the rail, seemingly oblivious to the damp cold, she said, "Norman, isn't the fog beautiful? There's something so soft and luxuriant about the way it caresses the buildings and the trees and casts them in a soft hue."

He looked where she was pointing. "Sure enough, it *was* beautiful, in a way," he says. "All of us commuters had chosen to focus on the negative aspects of the weather and were making ourselves miserable, whereas my mother found the good in it."

Learning Gratitude

If we wish to be more like that man's mother and less like the commuters, how do we go about changing? The answer does not lie in gritting our teeth and trying to block out the negatives. We can be governed by our admirations rather than our dislikes. We can concentrate so much on things for which we are grateful that there's no time to focus on gloom.

When I was a boy, we sang an old hymn with the refrain "Count your many blessings, name them one by one." It is one of the best ways to divest yourself of the negative: to consciously enumerate things for which you are grateful. When you are feeling sorry for yourself, Dale Carnegie recommends that you take out pencil and paper and make a list of all the good things you have, despite your problems.

Then in your mind, he advises, imagine each one of those things being taken away from you and what life would be like without them. When you've fully realized the emptiness, gradually give them back to yourself one by one, and you'll be surprised how much better you feel. Counting your blessings can be a stimulating exercise.

It is all the more important to exercise this habit of selection when our surroundings are unfavorable. The sculptress Louise Nevelson believed that one can live in great beauty anywhere. She made her home in the Bowery, New York City's skid row, and even there, she said, "I collect for my eye." Sitting in her dining room and looking out at the ugly building that stood across the street, she could find beauty in the varying patterns the sun and the moon reflected on its windows. She would look at a chair and say, "The chair isn't so hot, but look at its shadow."

The Power of the Thank You

Although Speaker of the House Sam Rayburn could be hard and ruthless in his political maneuvering, he was always warmly polite to waitresses and bellhops. A journalist once commented on this, and Rayburn said, "I wouldn't be unkind to a little boy or girl waiting on me for all the gold in Fort Knox. . . . What we do in this life is often determined by a mighty small margin. I missed being a tenant farmer by just that much"—he snapped his fingers—"but someone was kind to me in my youth."

Optimists, like Rayburn, seem to be sensitive to small acts of generosity from others. They are always saying "Thank you." They know that when they do so, it not only makes the other person feel good but also helps them keep their powers of admiration focused.

William Law, writing centuries ago, said, "Would you know who is the greatest saint in the world? It is not he

73

who prays most or fasts most, it is not he who lives most, but it is he who is always thankful to God, who receives everything as an instance of God's goodness and has a heart always ready to praise God for it."

Two Ways to Be Happy

Some people can think only of things they want: cars, vacations, new homes. Their minds are filled with want lists. But they are doomed to discontent, for no matter how much they acquire, there will always be things to envy in others. Someone has said that there are two ways to be happy: The first is to have the money to buy the things you would enjoy; the second is to have the wisdom to enjoy the things you have.

No one knew that wisdom more than the mother of Dr. Lee Salk, a child psychologist and professor of pediatrics at New York's Cornell University Medical College. He often refers to his mother's experiences growing up in Russia. As a girl, she was driven from her home by Cossacks. They burned the village to the ground, and she fled for her life, hiding in hay wagons and huddling in ditches. Eventually, crowded in a ship's hold, she crossed the sea to America.

Salk writes:

> Even after my mother married and her sons were born . . . it was still a struggle to keep food on the table. . . . But my mother urged us to think about what we *had*, not what we didn't have. She taught us that in hardship you develop a capacity to appreciate the beauty that exists in the simplest elements of life. The attitude that she so fiercely conveyed to us was this: "When it gets dark enough, you can see the stars."

Obsessed with Failure

A stocky young man once consulted me. He was disheartened, and with some reason, for he had recently failed the bar exam for the second time. He was out of money and said there was nothing left to live for.

"Nothing?" I asked.

"No. This is humiliating. They say that when you've flunked twice, the odds are that you'll never become a lawyer. I really don't have anything left to live for."

I took out a yellow pad and said, "I want to ask you a few questions about what you do have left. Are you married?"

"Yes, but that makes it worse. She's been terrific through this all, and I don't know why she stays with me when I'm such a failure."

"But does she love you?"

"I don't know how she could, but yes, she does."

I wrote that on the pad and then asked, "What about your parents? Are they alive?"

"My mom is. She's great. She was widowed when I was ten, and I couldn't ask for a better mother. That's another reason I'm so ashamed. She was so proud that I was going to be a lawyer. It would be better for all these people if I were dead."

"What about your health?" I asked. "Do you have any medical problems?"

"No, I seem to have a strong constitution. The morning of the bar exam the pressure was so intense that two students were vomiting on the steps of the building, but I've always been tough. Played football in college."

"Are you in any legal trouble?" I asked. "Have you done anything wrong, or is there any reason you might be arrested or get sent to jail?"

"No," he said, laughing for the first time. "I'm so square I've never even smoked marijuana. Not that being honest has got me anywhere, but at least I don't have to worry when I see a policeman."

"Do you believe in God?" I asked.

"Well, I'm not too big on church but I've always been big on God," he replied. "I never would have made it through law school without prayer."

"Do you think God loves you?" I asked.

"Oh sure, God loves me. I know that even when I've messed up like this."

"You seem like an ambitious guy," I commented. "Do you still have some dreams?"

"Oh yeah," he said. "I've always been a dreamer. That's what made me successful in football, even though I was the smallest guy on the team. I've got a lot of drive, and if I could just get past this exam, my wife and I have so many goals." He stared at the carpet and said, "There were so many great things we were going to enjoy."

I tore off the page and handed it to him. "It sounds as if when you stop and take inventory, you have quite a few good things left," I said.

I'd written on the page:

1. Wife loves him, won't give up on him.
2. Mother believes in him no matter what.
3. Health excellent; in fact, he's an athlete.
4. Thinks God loves him, believes in prayer.
5. Has lots of ambition—drive enabled him to succeed over obstacles as an athlete.

He stared at the list awhile and then raised his head and said, "That's amazing. I guess I was so obsessed with failing that exam that I couldn't see any hope."

I saw the young man for only a few more sessions, and

he went on his way. I wish I could report that he passed the bar exam on the next try, but he didn't. And he failed it again on his fourth try. But he would not give up and finally, on the fifth attempt, he passed. That happened several years ago, and I do not hear from him often, but he's a successful lawyer and businessman now despite that difficult start.

Savoring

No matter how bad their situation at the moment, optimists can always find things to enjoy—the smell of a wood-burning fireplace in the night air, the delight in a child's face while petting a kitten, the taste of a good cup of coffee.

The Vietnamese monk Thich Nhat Hanh lived through the long wars in Vietnam, helped victims of war, fed hungry children, and tried to ensure the safety of boat people on the turbulent Gulf of Siam. He is intimately acquainted with calamity, so he does not advocate trying to shut out pain, especially the pain of others: "Do not avoid contact with suffering or close your eyes before suffering. . . . Find ways to be with those who are suffering by all means, including personal contact and visits, images, sound. By such means, awaken yourself and others to the reality of suffering in the world."

But then he adds an important component to such pain:

> Life is filled with suffering, but it is also filled with many wonders, like the blue sky, the sunshine, the eyes of a baby. To suffer is not enough. We must also be in touch with the wonders of life. They are within us and all around us everywhere, any time . . . . Do we need to make a special effort to enjoy the beauty of the blue sky? Do we have to practice to be able to enjoy it? No, we just enjoy it . . . . Wherever we are,

any time, we have the capacity to enjoy the sunshine, the presence of each other, even the sensation of our breathing. We don't need to go to China to enjoy the blue sky. We don't have to travel into the future to enjoy our breathing. We can be in touch with these things right now. It would be a pity if we are only aware of suffering.

Thomas Merton wrote that Asian guides like Hanh have more carefully attended the subtle development of human spiritual consciousness than we normally have in the West.

David Leek, a retired dean of our local college, is a fine photographer and takes more than a thousand pictures a year. I once asked him, "Why do you always carry your camera? Are you trying to catch some freak accident and sell the negative to a magazine for a big price?"

"Oh, no," he answered. "I take pictures to help me see better. If I'm not careful, I can get lazy and fail to notice the new petals on our peach tree, or the colors in a lizard lounging on my patio. The camera helps keep my powers of observation sharp."

My wife is an expert at the art of admiration. Before we married, I do not once recall enjoying the taste of coffee in the morning. It was merely a lever to get me moving into the day. Then I met Diane, who, three mornings out of four, will hold her cup in both hands, inhale its aroma, and exclaim, "Oh, but that's good! I love the first cup of coffee."

So optimism is not saying that everything is getting better and better every day in every way. Nor is it saying that our worst days are behind us. We don't know either of those things. What we *do* know is that this world, for all its faults, is a big world filled with good things to be savored and enjoyed.

"As long as one can admire and love," said Pablo Casals, "then one is young forever."

*Our imagination is the only limit to
what we can hope to have in the future.*

CHARLES F. KETTERING

7 □ How to Predict the Future with Certainty

I once asked a man who is a world-class marksman about the qualities that make for success in that sport. "After you pass a certain level, the secret is mental conditioning," he said. "At first, of course, you've got to work hard to learn technique, and it's important to stay in good physical shape. But physical skill isn't as crucial as mental conditioning. We call it the three-pound powerhouse that sits on your shoulders. I can't get to the range every day, but I never let a day pass without playing a movie in my head in which I see myself shooting a perfect score. I take my time, and go through all the steps slowly in the imagination. Sometimes the repetition is boring, but it's essential to do it regularly."

Optimists are always doing what that marksman does. They vividly picture good things happening in the future. So the seventh characteristic is:

□ *Optimists use their imaginations to rehearse success.*

In the 1976 Olympics, Bruce Jenner won the gold medal for the decathlon, a grueling event that requires many diverse athletic skills and remarkable stamina. To what did Jenner attribute his success? "I always felt that my greatest asset was not my physical ability," he said. "It was my mental ability." Diver Greg Louganis, golfer Jack Nicklaus, and skater Scott Hamilton all take time to repetitiously visualize perfect dives, putts, and triple spins before they actually perform them.

Thinking with Images

Experiments show that for some sports, mental visioning seems to be more effective than actual practice. Alan Richardson had some subjects mentally practice a gymnastic exercise on the horizontal bar. They were asked to "see and feel themselves" moving through the activity for five minutes every day for six days before they attempted the actual exercise. Richardson expected that if imaging was an effective means of practice, then those with vivid imagery would perform better than those who had not done the exercises. That was exactly what happened.

Even more dramatic results came with two groups of people with equal ability for shooting free throw basketball shots. One group was required to practice every day; the other group was not allowed to practice, but spent time every day visualizing themselves shooting successful free throws. Sure enough, when the two groups competed, the visualizers were the winners.

Coach Bear Bryant won 323 college football games not only because he was a hard taskmaster with his players but also because he was a master painter of pictures. In his pre-game talks, he would help his players smell victory. He would describe to them what it was going to be like to see and feel the back slapping in the locker room after they'd won, to see the look in their parents' eyes, their girlfriends' embraces. With pictures like that playing within you, you tend to win a lot of games.

One corporation president reminisced about his first job: "I started my sales career by selling pots and pans from door to door. The first day I made only one sale in forty attempts. But I never forgot the face of that woman who finally bought something . . . how it changed from suspicion and hostility to gradual interest and final acceptance. For years I used to recall her face as a kind of talisman when the going was rough."

Many depressed people have changed their outlook simply by changing the use of their imagination. They learned to change the movies playing in their minds and began to substitute positive imaging for worry.

Worry

Worry is no more and no less than the misuse of imagination. Rather than using the imagination to play out happy events, the chronic worrier watches disasters and personal humiliations flashing on the inner screen.

The sad thing about such pictures is that most of those events are only faint possibilities. Mark Twain said he had known a lot of troubles in his life and most of them had never happened.

A businessman who was a chronic worrier decided to analyze his anxieties. He found that 40 percent of them were about things that were likely never to happen, 30 percent were about past decisions that could not be changed, 12 percent concerned criticism from others that didn't matter anyway, 10 percent were about his health (which he was already doing his best to protect), and only 8 percent were legitimate causes of worry. If we could eliminate our worries by 92 percent, we would be well on our way to solid self-possession.

Keeping Hope in the Future

Albert Einstein said that imagination is more important than knowledge. And indeed we do not give enough credit to the three-pound powerhouse sitting on our shoulders, for with its picture-making capacity it creates today what will happen tomorrow. Russell E. Palmer, dean of University of Pennsylvania's Wharton School, says that genuine leaders have an ability to visualize the big picture and that such a vision inspires people to follow them.

Palmer is right. Leaders are those who can look at a vacant lot and see a beautiful building, look at an empty church and visualize it overflowing with enthusiastic people, and take a demoralized group of workers and give them a vivid picture of what they could accomplish together.

The imagination has successfully sustained people who have had to keep faith for years in the most terrible circumstances. The years of the Vietnam War were a confused, troubled time for American foreign policy, making the suffering of the participants all the more tragic, but out of it has come a marvelous book, *Beyond Survival,* by U.S. Naval Captain Gerald L. Coffee. His plane was shot down over the China Sea on February 3, 1966, and he spent the next seven years in a succession of prison camps. The POWs who survived, he says, did so by a regimen of physical exercise, prayer, and stubborn communication with one another. After days of torture on the Vietnamese version of the rack, he signed the confession they demanded; then was thrown back into his cell to writhe in pain. Even worse was his guilt over having cracked. He did not know if there were other American prisoners in the cell block, but then he heard a voice: "Man in cell number 6 with the broken arm, can you hear me?"

It was Col. Robinson Risner. "It's safe to talk. Welcome to Heartbreak Hotel," he said.

"Colonel, any word about my navigator, Bob Hanson?" Coffee asked.

"No. Listen, Jerry, you must learn to communicate by tapping on the walls. It's the only dependable link we have to each other."

Risner had said "we"! That meant there were others. "Thank God, now I'm back with others," Coffee thought.

"Have they tortured you, Jerry?" Risner asked.

"Yes. And I feel terrible that they got anything out of me."

"Listen," Risner said, "once they decide to break a man, they do it. The important thing is how you come back. Just follow the Code. Resist to the utmost of your ability. If they break you, just don't stay broken. Lick your wounds and bounce back. Talk to someone if you can. Don't get down on yourself. We need to take care of one another."

For days at a time Coffee would be punished for some minor infraction, stretched on the ropes. His buddy in the next cell would tap on the wall, telling him to "hang tough," that he was praying for him. "Then, when he was being punished," Coffee says, "I would be on the wall doing the same for him."

At last, Coffee received a letter from his wife:

Dear Jerry,

It has been a beautiful spring but of course we miss you. The kids are doing great. Kim skis all the way around the lake now. The boys swim and dive off the dock, and little Jerry splashes around with a plastic bubble on his back.

Coffee stopped reading because his eyes were filling with tears as he clutched his wife's letter to his chest. "Little Jerry. Who's Jerry?" Then he realized. Their baby, born after his imprisonment, had been a son, and she had named him Jerry. There was no way she could know that all her previous letters had been undelivered, so she talked about their new son matter of factly. Coffee says:

Holding her letter, I was full of emotions: relief at finally knowing the family was well, sorrow for missing out on Jerry's entire first year, gratitude for the blessing of simply being alive. The letter concluded:

All of us, plus so many others, are praying for your safety and return soon. Take good care of yourself, honey.

I love you.

Bea

Coffee tells about the long, long hours during which the prisoners played movies in their minds of going from room to room in their houses back home, the camera taking in every detail. Over and over they played scenes of what it was going to be like to be back. Coffee says it was his friends and his faith that helped him through. Every Sunday the senior officer in each cell block would pass a signal – church call. Every man stood up in his cell, if he was able, and then with a semblance of togetherness, they would recite the Twenty-Third Psalm: "Thou preparest a table before me in the presence of mine enemies, thou anointest my head with oil; my cup runneth over." Coffee says:

> I realized that despite being incarcerated in this terrible place, it was *my* cup that runneth over, because someday, however, whenever, I would return to a beautiful and free country.

Finally, the peace treaty was signed, and on February 3, 1973, the seventh anniversary of his capture, Coffee was called before two young Vietnamese officers.

"Today it is our duty to return your belongings," one said.

"What belongings?" he asked.

"This."

He swallowed hard and reached for the gold wedding band the soldier held between his thumb and forefinger. Yes, it was his. He slipped it onto his finger. A little loose, but definitely his ring. He had never expected to see it again.

> [My] kids were eleven or twelve years old when my ring had been taken away. Suddenly I felt old and weary. During the prime years of my life, I had sat in a medieval dungeon, had my arm screwed up, had contracted worms and God knows what else. I wondered if my children, now older and changed so much, would accept me back into the family and what our reunion would be like. And I thought of Bea. Would I be okay for her? Did she still love me? Could she possibly know how much she had meant to me all these years?

The bus trip to the Hanoi airport was a blur, but one thing stood out with clarity for Coffee: the bright, beautiful, red, white, and blue flag painted on the tail of the enormous Air Force C-141 transport that gleamed in the sun, awaiting the first load of freed prisoners.

Next to the aircraft were several dozen American military people who smiled at them through the fence and gave them the thumbs-up signal. As they lined up by twos, the Vietnamese officer reeled off their names, rank, and service.

"Cmdr. Gerald L. Coffee, United States Navy" (he had been promoted two ranks in his absence).

As Coffee stepped forward, his attention was riveted on an American colonel wearing crisp Air Force blues, wings, and ribbons. It was the first American military uniform he had seen in many years. The colonel returned Coffee's brisk salute.

"Cmdr. Gerald Coffee reporting for duty, sir."

"Welcome back, Jerry." The colonel reached forward with both hands and shook Coffee's hand.

When the plane was loaded, the pilot taxied directly onto the runway without holding short, then locked the brakes and jammed his throttles forward. The huge beast rocked and vibrated as the pilot made his final checks of the engine's performance. The roar was horrendous as the brakes were released and they lurched forward on the runway. When they were airborne, the pilot's voice came up on the speaker and filled the cabin. It was a strong, sure voice.

"Congratulations, gentlemen. We've just left North Vietnam." Only then did they erupt into cheers.

The first leg of their trip home took them to Clark Air Force Base in the Philippines. The crowd held up banners: "Welcome Home! We love you, God bless." From behind the security lines they applauded wildly as the name of each debarking POW was announced. There were television cameras but the men had no idea that at that very moment in the small hours of the morning, millions of Americans back home were riveted to their television sets, cheering and weeping.

Special telephones had been set up to accommodate their initial calls home. Coffee's stomach churned as he waited the interminable few seconds for Bea to pick up the phone in Sanford, Florida, where she and the children were waiting.

"Hello, babe. It's me. Can you believe it?"

"Hi, honey. Yes. We watched you on TV when you came off the airplane. I think everybody in America saw you. You look great!"

"I dunno. I'm kinda scrawny. But I'm okay. I'm just anxious to get home."

After his long-awaited reunion with his wife and children, he and his family attended mass the following Sunday. Afterwards, in response to the parish priest's welcome, here is what Coffee said. It summarizes as well as anything I know the optimist's core:

Faith was really the key to my survival all those years. Faith in myself to simply pursue my duty to the best of my ability and ultimately return home with honor. Faith in my fellow man, starting with all of you here, knowing you would be looking out for my family, and faith in my comrades in those various cells and cell blocks in prison, men upon whom I depended and who in turn depended upon me, sometimes desperately. Faith in my country, its institutions and our national purpose and cause. . . . And, of course, faith in God—truly, as all of you know, the foundation for it all. . . . Our lives are a continuing journey—and we must learn and grow at every bend as we make our way, sometimes stumbling but always moving toward the finest within us.

*Action seems to follow feeling, but
really action and feeling go together.*

WILLIAM JAMES

8 □ The Difference Between Happiness and Cheerfulness

When her first child was about two years old, opera star Beverly Sills learned that the girl was almost totally deaf and would never hear the sound of her mother's voice. At almost the same time Sills gave birth to a second child, a son who proved to be autistic. The diva took a full year off to try to come to terms with her dual tragedy and to work with her daughter in a school for the deaf. Asked once if she was happy, she said, "I'm cheerful. There's a difference. A cheerful woman has cares but has learned how to deal with them."

Cheerfulness is something we can control much more than happiness. We can choose to behave cheerfully in dismal or dispiriting circumstances, in part to sustain our own strength, in part as an act of courtesy to the people we love. When we are miserable around them, we rob them of energy. Rather than pulling them down, we try to be cheerful in order to pull them up. Then an interesting thing begins to happen: We find ourselves feeling happier. The outward behavior influences the inward feelings.

William James, the dean of American psychologists, would not have been surprised at such a phenomenon. He was himself given to serious depression, but he found that we can counteract negative emotions by substituting the opposite behavior. Writing in 1892, he said, "By regulating the action . . . we can indirectly regulate the feeling. . . . Thus the sovereign voluntary path to cheerfulness, if our spontaneous cheerfulness be lost, is to sit up cheerfully . . . and to act and speak as if cheerfulness were already there."

The longer I've counseled people, the more I've come to believe that a moderate amount of denial can be salutary. When you're discouraged, it is remarkable how you can change your mood if you *act* enthusiastic.

So the seventh characteristic is:

☐ *Optimists are cheerful even when they can't be happy.*

At age ninety-three, Rose Kennedy is being interviewed by a magazine reporter. By this time, four of her nine children have died violently. Another daughter, Rosemary, has been severely retarded all her life and will soon be gone. Mrs. Kennedy has outlived her husband long enough to have seen his rather profligate and unscrupulous life told and retold in the press. She is an old lady, hit by tragedies again and again. The reporter asks about all this and Rose Kennedy says, slowly: "I have always believed that God never gives a cross to bear larger than we can carry. And I have always believed that, no matter what, God wants us to be happy. He doesn't want us to be sad. Birds sing after a storm. Why shouldn't we?"

Those words are the brave declaration of a woman who has determined that she will be cheerful even when her situation is not happy.

The "As-If" Principle

Lincoln Kirstein, the crusty director of the New York City Ballet, learned this principle from the mystic, Gurdjieff. Kirstein once wrote, "He gave me a method which can be lightly called 'as if.' You behave 'as if' something were true. Then you make it happen. We thought of a ballet school, a company, Lincoln Center, long before they happened. By behaving as if it would happen, we wasted no time."

C. S. Lewis once advised that if you don't feel love for another person, act as if you do, and the emotion will often follow the behavior; you will find yourself feeling, if not love, at least more sympathy and affection. Couples in a troubled marriage can accomplish a lot of good simply by doing thoughtful things for each other and acting in a loving and tender manner. Such action may not only elicit more love from your mate—it also may change how you feel inside.

But Can We Really Be Happier By Pretending to Be So?

There is a built-in danger in this "as-if" principle. In trying to act cheerful one can become artificial. The people we enjoy usually have an honest range of emotions, rather than paste-on smiles. But it is not dishonest for people to lift themselves out of depression by behaving enthusiastically. Those who attend aerobic classes may not feel in a good mood when the music starts, but once they begin to exercise to the beat with energetic expressions, it is remarkable how their moods change to fit their actions. Michael Campos, who runs a school of martial arts in Johnstown, New York, uses this principle in his teaching. "The typical karate yell has three purposes," he says. "It tightens the stomach muscles, scares the opponent, and, most important, helps people feel confident."

Many of us already apply this practical psychology without realizing it. "Smile," we urge a tearful child, and unwillingly the child smiles—and is cheered up. As a demonstration of this idea at a workshop, Nathaniel Branden had a group of us stand, put our hands high in the air, and jump up and down. Then, as we were jumping, he asked us to repeat, "I feel depressed! I'm in a bad mood!" We found it almost impossible to do. Either we had to stop the energetic body movements to say, "I feel depressed," or we had to stop saying "I feel depressed" to move our bodies so energetically.

Here are some guidelines for maintaining a cheerful demeanor.

Guideline # 1: Begin the Day Well

A businessman says that some mornings he gets up feeling sluggish and unenthusiastic about going to work. However, he has a habit of doing calisthenics in his bedroom before showering, and that helps his spirits. "Next," he says, "I do what I call spiritual calisthenics. This may sound a little crazy, but I repeat aloud several Bible verses I've memorized, and I do it in a strong, enthusiastic voice, even when I'm not feeling cheerful or enthusiastic. For instance, I look out the bedroom window and repeat the verse from the Psalms, 'This is the day which the Lord hath made. I will rejoice and be glad in it.' It may be raining, and I may have been dreading the pile of work on my desk, but when I do these exercises it's amazing how much more optimistic I feel."

This ability—to move in the opposite direction from the one to which our mood is leading—is one worth cultivating. Former U.S. Congressman Ed Foreman says that a sure way to stay in a bad mood all day is to get up late, skip breakfast, and tear off to work at a breakneck pace. He suggests getting up early enough to fill the first few minutes with some good inspirational reading or listening to a motivational tape with ideas you'd like to keep with you all day. "Then slip on some comfortable clothes," he says, "and go out and watch the morning wake up."

Guideline # 2: Employ the Therapy of Laughter

One clear-cut characteristic of optimists is that they never take themselves too seriously. Many recent studies show that when people laugh enough each day, they find their emotions running on a more optimistic track. Here again, we ordinarily assume that the action follows the feeling, that people will laugh when they are happy. But it often works the other way. When people laugh enough, their inner feelings of despondency or discouragement begin to lift.

Norman Cousins, seriously ill in the hospital, decided to move to a hotel room, where he submitted himself to what he called laugh therapy—watching old Marx Brothers films and "Candid Camera" tapes. He found that ten minutes of solid belly laughter would give him two hours of pain-free sleep. Because his illness involved severe inflammation of the spine and joints, making it painful to turn over in bed, the practical value of laughter became very important to him. A number of subsequent studies have accumulated to support the biblical proverb "A cheerful heart is a good medicine" and Aristotle's remark that "laughter is a bodily exercise precious to health."

Norman Cousins had seen the power of laughter long before, when he made many visits to Dr. Albert Schweitzer's famous hospital in Lambaréné. He writes:

> Schweitzer employed humor as a form of equatorial therapy, a way of reducing the temperatures and the humidity and the tensions. His use of humor, in fact, was so artistic that one had the feeling he almost regarded it as a musical instrument.
>
> Life for the young doctors and nurses was not easy. . . . Dr. Schweitzer knew it and gave himself the task of supplying nutrients for their spirits. At mealtimes, when the staff came together, Schweitzer always had an amusing story or two to go with the meal. Laughter at the dinner hour was probably the most important course. It was fascinating to see the way the staff members seemed to be rejuvenated by the wryness of his humor.

Dr. William Fry, Jr., of Stanford Medical School, compares laughter to a form of physical exercise. It causes huffing and puffing, accelerates the heart rate, raises blood pressure, speeds up breathing, increases oxygen consumption, gives the muscles of the face and stomach a workout, and relaxes muscles not involved in laughing. Liver, stomach, pancreas, spleen, and gall bladder are all stimulated. In short, your entire system gets an invigorating lift.

Some of us have our noses so pressed to the grindstone that opportunities for these fleeting moments of pleasure pass us by. Yet if laughter is as important an antidote for depression as studies indicate, the person who wants to move from pessimism to optimism will be well advised to build some time for fun into every day. I know a woman who is a partner in an interior design firm that employs several artists— the sort of place where one would expect to find prima donnas who have trouble getting along. This company has a remarkable morale, and the employees seem to genuinely enjoy working with one another. When I watch this woman go to work each morning (she happens to be my wife), I see some of the reason for that company's esprit de corps. She leaves determined to get along with people, to give and receive some love, and to have fun and laugh during the day.

Richard Hanser, writing about Lincoln's Civil War years, says, "Humor was his bulwark against the bitter and bloody disasters of the Civil War. His gaunt, towering figure, clad in flapping flannel nightgown, used to stalk through the White House at midnight seeking someone still awake to share a funny story he had just read."

Hanser goes on to say that on September 22, 1862, the War Cabinet was summoned to the White House for a special session. "The president was reading a book and hardly noticed me as I came in," Secretary of War Stanton wrote later. "Finally he turned to us and said: 'Gentlemen, did you ever read anything of Artemus Ward? Let me read a chapter that is very funny.'"

The president then read aloud a skit called *High-Handed Outrage at Utica*. Stanton was furious, but Lincoln read on, and at the end laughed heartily. "Gentlemen," he asked, "why don't you laugh? With the fearful strain that is upon me night and day, if I did not laugh, I should die, and you need this medicine as much as I do."

Then he reached into his tall hat on the table and pulled

out a paper from which he read. It was the Emancipation Proclamation. Stanton was overwhelmed. He got up, took Lincoln's hand, and said: "Mr. President, if reading a chapter of Artemus Ward is a prelude to such a deed as this, the book should be filed among the archives of the nation and the author canonized."

Guideline # 3: Insist on Celebrations Even During Hard Times

British physician Sheila Cassidy writes in a touching way about the importance of laughter and celebration in a hospice:

> Although medically speaking, hospices exist to provide a service of pain and symptom control for those for whom active anticancer treatment is no longer appropriate—there is *always* something that can be done for the dying, even if it's only having the patience and the courage to sit with them. Most lay people imagine that hospices are solemn, rather depressing places where voices are hushed and eyes downcast as patients and their families await the inevitable. Nothing could be further from the truth. Hospice care is about life and love and laughter, for it is founded upon two unshakable beliefs: that life is so precious that each minute should be lived to the full, and that death is quite simply a part of life, to be faced openly and greeted with the hand outstretched. One of the hallmarks of hospice life is celebration: Cakes are baked and champagne uncorked at the first hint of a birthday or anniversary, and administrators, nurses, and volunteers clink glasses with patients and their families.

Guideline # 4: Employ Uplifting Music to Lift Your Mood

Why do Japanese companies have their employees sing and do calisthenics each day before they start to work?

Because the managers have learned that such exercises can alter the workers' attitudes. Music can be an important stimulant to optimistic thinking. Churches have always included singing in worship, and music is more effective when the whole congregation sings rather than when they listen to a choir perform. Singing reinforces one's beliefs.

Dr. Donn Moomaw told his congregation about a visit to Aspen, Colorado. "Even in that beautiful setting," he reported, "walking on a snowy street early in the morning, I felt down. I tried several things to get myself out of the dark mood, and nothing worked until I tried singing. It wasn't very good music—simple church songs in the voice of an ex-football player. But when I started singing—when my emotions got beyond words and into music—I began to feel better."

A young man was fired from his first job and was sure the end of the world had come. "With the pessimism of youth, I was convinced that I would never find another job. I was marked for failure. That evening I had a date to meet a friend to hear the New York Philharmonic. Job or no job, I decided to go. At first . . . the music merely lapped against the stone wall of my anxiety. But with the final number of the program, the First Symphony of Brahms, I began to listen in earnest. I measured the event of the day more calmly. Was it as important as all that? Couldn't I do something about it? As I walked home, the dull blanket of despondency weighed less. Somehow I would manage to find another job." The young man did find a new job soon and went on to considerable accomplishments.

When King Saul was depressed, he frequently summoned the young David to play the harp for him, and his melancholy lifted. Horace spoke of music as "the healing balm of troubles." Congreve in *The Mourning Bride* said, "Music hath charms to soothe the savage breast." Coleridge said, "I feel physically refreshed and strengthened by it."

☐ *Optimists are cheerful even when they can't be happy.*

And Goethe, who was not particularly musical, said music made him unfold "like the fingers of a threatening fist which straighten amicably."

Guideline # 5: Take a Brisk Walk

One of the best antidotes for depression is vigorous physical exercise. For some depressives, I conduct our therapy session while we walk the streets near my office. They often resist this unorthodox approach and tell me that they're far too depressed and tired to get out of the chair. Sometimes I must say, "Well, let's try walking one block. Then if it's too much, we'll come back." Once out and moving, they're usually surprised at how much better they feel, and we walk for the entire hour.

Robert Thayer, a researcher at California State, Long Beach, recently took a visitor to the college cafeteria. "They are stoking up on sweet rolls and coffee," he pointed out, "buying Twinkies in an attempt to get themselves 'up' for their 9:30 A.M. classes. What they don't know is that they are being counterproductive." In one study, Thayer compared eating a candy bar with taking a brisk, ten-minute walk. Although both strategies had a mood-elevating result, the people who ate the candy were even more tired and tense an hour later. On the other hand, those who had taken the brisk walk sustained their heightened mood.

This brings us to an interesting question we need to consider before leaving this subject. Do optimists have better health because of their attitude, or are they optimists because they happen to be healthy?

Christopher Peterson, a University of Michigan psychologist, measured the amount of optimism and pessimism in 172 people, then questioned them a year later about infectious diseases. He found a strong correlation between pessimism and subsequent illness. The pessimists reported twice as many illnesses and doctors' visits during the year as did the optimists.

Dr. George E. Vaillant has been following the physical and mental health of several hundred Harvard graduates since the mid 1940s. The data includes the results of extensive physical exams done every five years from age twenty-five through sixty. Ninety-nine of the men were rated by researchers as pessimistic, and they had markedly more illness between forty-five and sixty than the optimists. Curiously, a man's attitude at age twenty-five does not seem to affect his health for about twenty years. But if he has a robust body and good health at twenty-five, and also carries a bleak and cynical attitude, the researchers can predict that his health will begin to fall apart at middle age.

Other researchers studied a much more serious matter—sixty-nine women who had mastectomies for breast cancer. Three months after the surgery the women were asked how they viewed the nature and seriousness of the disease and how it had affected their lives. Five years later 75 percent of the women who had reacted with a positive, fighting spirit were alive, whereas less than half of those who reacted either stoically or helplessly were still alive.

Does this prove that you can cure cancer with a positive attitude? No, of course not. Lots of optimists die of cancer, and it will be a long time before all the data is in on the relationships between mind and body. In this research, for instance, it is not entirely clear what is cause and what is effect. Do pessimists bring trouble on themselves? Or do they become pessimistic because they have diseases like cancer? We do have hard data showing that pessimists smoke and drink more, and exercise less, than optimists. So it becomes the same question that has intrigued psychologists for a long while: Do our patients live the way they do because of their demons, or do they have those demons because they live the way they do?

□ *Optimists are cheerful even when they can't be happy.*

It is doubtless a two-way street. When people have a troubled life, it gives them good cause to be pessimistic. On the other hand, research shows that pessimists make a mess of their lives and fail to do the things they could to remedy their situations. So for the person who wants to become more optimistic, the question of cause and effect is really academic. The fact is that we can improve our moods by such simple acts as taking a brisk walk, we can improve our health by acting the way healthy people act, and we can become more optimistic by being cheerful. William James was right: "Action may seem to follow feeling, but really action and feeling go together."

I could not at any age be content to take my place in a corner by the fireside and simply look on. Life was meant to be lived. One must never, for whatever reason, turn one's back on life.

ELEANOR ROOSEVELT

To have succeeded is to have finished one's business on earth, like the male spider who is killed by the female the moment he has succeeded in his courtship. I like a state of continual becoming, with a goal in front and not behind.

GEORGE BERNARD SHAW

9 □ Developing Your Capacities

Another character trait that marks off the optimists from the rest of the world is this: Regardless of their age, they have a stubborn belief that their personal best is yet to be. Characteristic number nine then is:

☐ *Optimists believe they have an almost unlimited capacity for stretching.*

Perhaps the greatest value of sports is what such activities teach us about our ability to extend ourselves. With rigorous training our bodies can be stretched and conditioned so that in a remarkably short time they are capable of more than we would have imagined. In earlier years some experts made the mistake of saying that the limit of speed or strength or endurance for the human body had been reached, and no new records would be set in some sport. Experts no longer make such remarks, because someone keeps coming along to set a new world record. For instance, of the many important indices of women's progress in recent years probably none is so dramatic as the 2 hours 25 minutes 30 seconds in which Ingrid Kristiansen ran the 1989 New York Marathon. Not only did Mrs. Kristiansen's time make her the first woman to finish that day, but it also meant that in just twenty years the women's record had been improved *by more than one hour.* Her time was faster than that of half of all the male winners of the Olympic marathon, and of *all* the men who ran in the 1970 New York Marathon.

The Brain's Capacities for Expansion

The brain has much occupied the attention of Lewis Thomas, M.D., a polished essayist who for many years was president of New York's Sloan-Kettering Cancer Center. In

Medusa and the Snail he contemplates the joining of a solitary sperm and egg that grows into eight pounds of baby. The real amazement, he says, is that each of us starts out as a single cell, then divides into two, then four, then eight, and at a certain stage there emerges one cluster of cells that will have as its progeny the human brain.

"The mere existence of those special cells," Thomas writes, "should be one of the great astonishments of the earth. One group of cells is switched on to become the whole trillion-cell, massive apparatus for thinking and imagining. All the information needed for learning to read and write, and play the piano."

The brain's capacity is almost inexhaustible. No one is sure how many cells the brain contains, but estimates range from ten to twelve billion, each of which has a set of microscopic tendrils that pass electrochemical messages from one cell to another. As you have been reading this page, millions of these switches have been going on and off to make it possible for you to assimilate these ideas, connect them with your past experiences, form pictures, and file the data away. Dr. Ralph W. Gerary, neurophysiologist at the University of Michigan, once estimated that after seventy years of activity, the brain may contain as many as fifteen trillion separate bits of information.

Warts and the Power of the Mind

Optimists do not believe that their minds are necessarily better than other people's. They believe that we *all* have minds capable of accomplishing remarkable things.

Take the simple wart. Several meticulous studies by expert clinical investigators show that warts can be made to disappear by something that can only be called thinking. In one study, fourteen patients with seemingly intractable warts on both sides of the body were hypnotized. The suggestion was given that all the warts on one side of the body would go away. Within several weeks the results were indisputably positive. In nine patients, all or nearly all of the warts on the suggested side had vanished, while the control side had as many as ever.

Discussing this study, Lewis Thomas says he has been trying to figure out the nature of the instructions issued by the unconscious mind that would send specific orders for deploying the various classes of lymph cells in the correct order to remove one set of warts, while making sure at the same time that the warts on the other side of the body were left intact. Lewis says he can only conclude "that my unconscious is a lot further along than I am."

Optimism and the Senior Years

This data about the capacity of the human mind and body for expansion has a great deal of relevance to the treatment of depression in older people. Fifteen percent of seniors suffer from depression, double the figure for the whole population. This is not surprising, because as we grow older, we can become obsessed with the things we can no longer do. Unquestionably there is some reduction of powers as we age. The body, for instance, loses some of its agility. But if we were going to bemoan those losses, we should have begun long ago. Our eyes began to age at ten; our hearing around twenty. By thirty our muscular strength, reaction time, and reproductive powers have all passed their peak. On the other hand, our minds can still be young at fifty. And at eighty we can be more productive mentally than at thirty because we possess something we didn't have at thirty: experience.

The *Wall Street Journal* tells how Harry Lipsig, at age eighty-eight, decided to leave the New York law firm he had spent most of sixty years building up (and where he was earning $5 million a year) to open a new firm. There had been some differences with his younger partners who questioned his ability to handle lengthy court trials. (One judge recalls Mr. Lipsig saying that he wasn't dying fast enough for his partners.)

So in 1988, Mr. Lipsig decided to try personally his first case in some time. Here is the *Journal*'s analysis:

> The plaintiff was suing the city of New York because a drunken police officer had struck and killed her seventy-one-year-old husband with his patrol car. She was . . . arguing that the city had deprived her of her husband's future earnings potential. The city argued that at age 71, he had little earnings potential. What better evidence for the plaintiff than the presence in court of a vigorous eighty-eight-year-old attorney? The city settled the case for $1.25 million.

Lipsig started his new firm with only one partner and an executive assistant. In his makeshift office, outfitted with seventeen phone lines, Mr. Lipsig says he couldn't be happier. His memory isn't what it once was, he concedes, but assistants sit in on client meetings to remind him of things, and he says he has lined up several other firms to help him with cases as co-counsel.

Retire? Never, he says. A few doctors have recommended it along the way, he notes with a smile, but they're all dead now.

Samuel Ullman has said that nobody grows old merely by living a number of years; people grow old by deserting their ideals. Optimists do not allow themselves to be obsessed with the losses of age. They are obsessed with the new thing they're learning, the new skill they're acquiring, the new project they're supporting. They usually like what they're doing for a living, and they have large enterprises for the future. When they retire, it's only to change occupations.

□ *Optimists think they have an almost unlimited capacity for stretching.*

Konrad Adenauer, who at eighty was still chancellor of West Germany, was once laid low by a siege of the grippe. His physician told him, "I'm not a magician. I can't make you young again." Eager to get back into harness, Adenauer replied, "I'm not asking that. I don't want to become young again. All I want is to go on getting older."

The Dilemma of Fading Beauty

Perhaps the toughest struggles with aging are waged by athletes and actors, the "beautiful people" who have made their mark with physical prowess or glamour. There is nothing sadder than an over-the-hill athlete who has let his body go and knows that his day is past. Or an actress whose youthful image still appears on late-night movies but who no longer wants to be seen in public because the years have taken their toll.

Sophia Loren, who by age fifty had been in seventy-five films, said, "There *is* a fountain of youth: It is your mind, your talents, the creativity you bring in your life and the lives of people you love. . . . Today, women are doing things that their mothers would never have dreamed of doing. I consider myself very fortunate to be living in a time when there is always a future for a woman, no matter what her age."

Browning's poem "Rabbi Ben Ezra" has a couplet that says,

Grow old along with me,
The best is yet to be.

Some cynics scoff at such talk and say that Browning knew nothing about the hell of old age. I decided to test this idealism on a friend whom I admire a great deal and who, at eighty-three, claims that she "keeps five different medical specialists busy." I read her the poem and asked if she thought it mere sentimentalism.

She sat and thought a moment. "Oh, maybe Browning overstated it a little," she said. "Old age is not for sissies." Then a twinkle came into her eye. "But I'll tell you one thing," she said, leaning forward. "I'd rather spend these years with a man who says, 'Come grow old with me, the best is yet to be,' than with some crotchety old fellow who can only sit by the window and curse his fate."

Love becomes the ultimate answer
to the ultimate human question.

ARCHIBALD MACLEISH

10 □ How Love Nurtures Optimism

When they are depressed, many people withdraw, pull the shades, twist into a cocoon, and stop seeing their friends. This is the worst possible thing to do. When asked what is the best inducement of positive moods, clinical psychologist Lee Anna Clark of Southern Methodist University replied, "I couldn't believe this, but it held true for all my subjects. It turns out that when people were socializing, about 82 percent of the time they reported being in a better mood."

Reflecting on the strongly optimistic people I know, I'm struck by the depth and scope of their relationships. How they love! They love many things passionately—sports, nature, music. But most of all they love people. They respond to children with enthusiasm, they are profoundly connected to their families, they respond to people in trouble, they touch a lot and make love a lot. This ability to admire and enjoy others is a powerful force that helps account for their optimism.

So characteristic number nine is:

□ *Optimists build lots of love into their lives.*

It is not original with me to observe that love is found not so much by those who are good-looking or witty or who have charismatic personalities, but rather by those who devote attention to love, who value it when they find it, and who nurture its growth in long-standing relationships. "Love never dies of a natural death," Anaïs Nin once wrote. "It dies because we don't know how to replenish its source; it dies of blindness and errors and betrayals. It dies of illness and wounds; it dies of weariness, of witherings, of tarnishings." And the author Robert Anderson says of love in marriage: "In every marriage more than a week old, there are grounds for divorce. The trick is to find, and continue to find, grounds for marriage."

Historian Will Durant describes how he looked for happiness in knowledge, travel, wealth, only to be disappointed. Then one day, riding a train, he saw a quick vignette. A woman was waiting in a tiny car with a sleeping child in her arms. A man got off the train, walked to the car, and gently kissed the woman and then the baby, very softly so as not to waken him. Then the family drove off together and left Durant with the stunning realization that "every normal function of life holds some delight."

When Adm. Richard E. Byrd believed himself to be dying in the Antarctic ice of the Ross Barrier, he wrote some thoughts on happiness: "I realized I had failed to see that the simple, homely, unpretentious things of life are the most important. When a man achieves a fair measure of harmony within himself and his family circle, he achieves peace. At the end only two things really matter to a man, regardless of who he is: the affection and understanding of his family."

Bill Cosby was twenty-six when, after one year as a marginally employable comedian, he married a nineteen-year-old university student, Camille Hanks—beautiful, intelligent, cultured, talented, and just as strong-willed as Cosby. A family friend says, "She's the wind beneath his wings."

"My life now," Cosby says, "is a very happy one. It's a happiness of being deeply connected, of knowing there is someone I can trust completely, and that the one I trust is the one I love. With her strength and help, I can only become better, and I want to because"—his voice breaks—"I want her to be proud of me."

The Necessity of Love

The unconnected self is an impotent thing, so the desire to love and be loved is no more selfish than breathing. Lisa Berkman and her colleagues at the University of California in Berkeley made an intensive study of seven thousand adults over nine years. They found that people with weak social ties had a death rate two to five times higher than those with strong social ties. A study conducted at the University of Syracuse investigated the health habits of four hundred adult citizens of Rockford, Illinois. It found that people who frequently visited with friends and neighbors were more likely to have good health habits than those who spent little time with others.

In an Israeli study, ten thousand married men forty years of age or older were tracked for five years. The researchers, Jack H. Medalie and Uri Goldbourt, wanted to find out how new cases of angina pectoris, a form of heart attack, developed. They assessed each man's medical risk factors for heart disease and then asked, among other items on a questionnaire, "Does your wife show you her love?" The answer turned out to have enormous predictive power. Among high-risk men—men who showed elevated blood cholesterol, electrocardiographic abnormalities, and high levels of anxiety—those who had loving and supportive wives developed fewer cases of angina pectoris than those whose wives were colder (52 per 1,000 versus 93 per 1,000).

The Therapy of Serving

What do we mean by the love that nurtures optimism? Such love is far more than seeking relationships that will nourish us. To be genuine, love also desires to nourish others. I often try to put depressed patients in contact with someone they can help, for there is something therapeutic about doing another person a favor. "Life is an exciting business," Helen Keller once said, "and it is most exciting when it is lived for others."

A wise minister I know was consulted by a widow who was feeling very sorry for herself at Thanksgiving time because she was alone and depressed. The pastor said, "I'm going to give you a prescription," and proceeded to write on a slip of paper the name and address of an old couple who were poor and ill with the flu. "These people are a lot worse off than you," he said bluntly. "Go do something for them."

The woman went away muttering, but the next day she took a cab to the address she'd been given. There, in a tiny apartment, she found the couple. They were barely able to fix meals for each other and were frightened that one of them would have to enter a nursing home. So the woman arranged to take them Thanksgiving dinner. When she came back to see the minister the following week, she had new bounce to her step. "I hadn't fixed a turkey in years," she said. "But I shopped for all the trimmings and got up at 5:00 A.M. to put the bird in. When the taxi driver and I took it in to them, it was the best Thanksgiving I'd had in years."

Oscar-winning screenwriter Robert Towne tells how his career hit bottom with a thud in 1982. At the same time, he was involved in a bitter custody battle with his ex-wife, and depressed by the death of a dog to which he had been "shamelessly attached."

"I walked out on a desolate beach filled with garbage from Santa Monica Bay and felt I had nothing left," Towne says. "There was a guy on the beach with his wife and he came up to me and said, 'Excuse me, but we made a mistake. We came out here, but because of the bus strike our transfer tickets don't work and we can't get back downtown. Can you help us?' I reached into my pocket and gave him all the money I had.

"I realized that this was the best thing anybody could have done for me. I was feeling completely impotent, and here on this beach was one guy I could do something for. It made me feel that I was not completely useless, that somehow things would be O.K."

Love Outside Marriage

I do not mean to imply that one must be married with children in order to be happy. It helps to have an extended family who care about one another and look out for one another, but that's not possible for everyone. Hence friendship is very important for mental health. I see many people distance themselves from friends when they are depressed. Their loneliness makes them increasingly disagreeable, and their disagreeableness drives friends away. This process becomes a vicious downward spiral. On the other hand, most of us can take any defeat if we have some people who love us. So it is essential that we keep our friendships in repair, as Dr. Samuel Johnson advised, and that we regularly make new friends to replace the ones who drift away for various reasons.

We can live without sex, we can live without having a family, but we cannot live without love.

Cynics do not create.

CALVIN COOLIDGE

11 □ How Optimists Cope with Hostility

"I think I married the wrong guy," said the young woman in my office. "We've only been married two years, and our marriage is on the rocks."

When I began to gather a little information about their disagreements and disputes, it became clear that she had not married the wrong person at all. This couple simply needed to learn how to express negative emotions without destroying their relationship. People cannot live together in the same house or be thrown together anywhere for many hours a week without bumping into each other a great deal and occasionally stepping on each other's toes.

The Difference Between Hostility and Anger

Since love is such a necessary ingredient for building optimism, we must devote a few more pages to the topic before going on to the next characteristic. In particular, we will talk about such impediments to love as hostility and faultfinding.

A host of recent studies say the same thing: People who are chronically hostile, who see the world through a lens of suspicion and cynicism, not only leave behind them a trail of carnage but also shorten their own lives. Hostility is suicidal, according to Redford Williams, M.D., an internist and behavioral medicine researcher at Duke University Medical Center. Thirty years ago two San Francisco cardiologists, Dr. Meyer Freidman and Dr. Ray H. Rosenman coined the term *Type A* to describe a person who is ambitious, competitive, always in a hurry, fiercely focusing on work. Such a person, their research showed, was more prone to heart disease.

Many of us had our doubts about that research, because it seemed obvious that people who stay busy and have an intense dedication to their work are usually happy and healthy. Now Williams's work sharpens the earlier research considerably. He shows that it is primarily one group of Type A people who are at risk: angry, hostile people. Using the Minnesota Multiphasic Personality Inventory (M.M.P.I.), a widely used psychological test that measures, among other things, the level of one's hostility, he found that hostile medical students were five times more likely to have a heart attack than those who were not hostile. A similar study looked at 118 lawyers who had taken the M.M.P.I. as students at the University of North Carolina School of Law. Those who scored highest on the hostility scale were 4.2 times more likely to have died three decades later from heart disease or other causes.

The Antidote to Hostility

If you feel hostility, what should you do about it? The answer does not lie in trying to live without any anger, swallowing all your frustration. None of the research suggests that it is unhealthy to display anger from time to time. In modern life many situations arise that are bound to cause frustration with other people, and expressing it in an appropriate manner can be good for one's health. The problem arises, says Dr. Williams, when hostility is chronic, when it becomes a regular personal style.

The antidote is to develop what Williams calls a trusting heart, and he outlines twelve steps to develop a more amiable disposition. Some of the steps are obvious, such as learning to relax with meditation, but a surprisingly large number of his suggestions are patterned after the cognitive therapy we discussed in an earlier chapter. People who learn to listen to their thoughts and discover themselves harboring vindictive, critical evaluations of others—habitual ways of thinking about others that make us pessimists—can substitute more reasonable responses. For instance, if an elevator takes a long time to come, think of a good reason why it may have stopped along the way rather than rage against some imaginary person's thoughtlessness in holding it up. Try to see things from the other person's point of view, says Williams. Empathy can soothe the troubled heart.

What we're really discussing here is the virtue of tolerance. I once saw hanging on a monastery wall this saying: "Love comes to those who are able to accept human nature as it is." When Jesus urged that we not take the speck out of our neighbor's eye until we deal with the log in our own, he was asking us to laugh at ourselves — at our tendency to be so bothered by the frailties of others when we have frailties ourselves — sometimes much more grievous ones. The more relaxed we become with our imperfection, the more tolerant we will become of the world at large.

The Power to Understand

In Dr. Williams's list of ways hostile people can free themselves of stress, he uses a category one does not usually hear from cardiologists. He recommends forgiveness:

> Rather than blame those who have mistreated you, rather than continuing to resent them and to seek revenge, try to understand the emotions of the one who has wronged you. By letting go of the resentment and relinquishing the goal of retribution, you may find . . . that the weight of anger lifts from your shoulders, easing your pain and also helping you to forget the wrong.

All of us have trouble forgiving people, especially those who are unlovable and keep repeating their mistakes against us. (The irony is that these unlovable people are the ones who need love the most.) Williams is on to something very important here when he urges us to try to understand the emotions of the person who has wronged us. For understanding and love are not two things, but one. We have all had the experience of being repulsed by people at first meeting, but then, as we learned more of their history and came to know other facets of their personalities, we tolerated them much better, and in some instances, even learned to love them.

Robert Fulghum, the wise author of books like *All I Really Need to Know I Learned in Kindergarten*, says that the more we get to know about human nature, the more likely we are to give people the benefit of the doubt. He says he is often surprised to see a couple of fat, homely types get up on the floor and waltz like angels. "When I see people like that on the street," he writes, "and start to look down my nose at them, a better voice in my head says, 'Probably dancers,' and I feel better about them. And me."

Motivating Your Employees

When I speak to corporate groups and meet CEOs or managers who are successful, I always ask their secret, and with remarkable frequency they give the same answer: "I have good people working for me."

The puzzle, then, is, are these leaders more successful because they know how to find talented people when other managers do not? Perhaps that's a little of their secret, but much more important, I think, is a fundamental view of human nature behind that remark. They believe in people, they enjoy working with people, and they take great pleasure in building others up. The result is a fierce loyalty from their staff.

Some get to be managers quickly because of their self-discipline, but then they have trouble working with employees who do not share that drive. It is easy to get angry with a staff member by thinking, "Why doesn't he get off the dime and do what I ask him to do? He's got more excuses for lousy production than anybody I've ever worked with. He must sit at his desk and deliberately think of ways to frustrate me! I wonder what it would take to get him fired?"

Such a train of thought, even if pursued for a short time, can cause a usually rational person to erupt in unreasonable anger and wreak havoc on an already fragile relationship. A better line of thought would be: "Now there's got to be a way to build a fire under that guy. He's bright, and he'd probably like to succeed in this job as much as I want him to. For the time being, then, I'm going to assume he has good intentions and wants to get out of this slump. If I fired him and hired a new person, we could have the same problems again. I should ask what he thinks the difficulty is before I jump to any conclusions. Maybe we can put our heads together and figure out a way to get him motivated."

Practical optimists are not suckers, and they are not taken in by people, but they have a way of bringing out the best in people.

A Belief in the Human Species

The best leaders have a very high view of the dignity of the individual. Unfortunately, when some people get older or when they have had several years' experience in the service professions, they can get cynical about human nature and forget to respect the dignity of each individual. One sees it often in marketing people, and it is even prevalent among ministers, teachers, and psychotherapists. In supervising young therapists, I worry about the ones who with a certain condescension assign labels to their patients. Perhaps they are merely trying to sound sophisticated, but these therapists do not seem very interested in the *stories* of their people, and that is a bad sign.

On the other hand, I watch my partner, Dr. Taz Kinney, who has been practicing medicine for almost forty years, first as a family physician and then as a psychiatrist. He is the most rigorous diagnostician I know, yet after all these years of working with disturbed patients (many from second- and third-generation welfare families), he continues to be genuinely interested in the everyday details of their lives. I know this because I am sometimes standing at the coffee machine as he ushers a new patient into his office, and I hear the way he greets them, and the humorous banter that goes on as he prepares to give them an injection. It is evident that he finds things about them to enjoy and admire, and he is not affronted when they do not all get well. Some of the younger therapists in our office come in with a messianic plan to cure everyone, and they can get very frustrated when their patients do not improve at the rate they expect. Having been a family doctor, Dr. Kinney is much more patient, and he sometimes quotes the motto from a country doctor's office. It read:

The doctor's job:

- To cure occasionally
- To help frequently
- To comfort always

A long-awaited study by the National Institute of Mental Health has some surprising revelations about the comparative effectiveness of various types of psychotherapy for depressed patients. Four types of therapy were compared in a long study using twenty-eight therapists and 250 patients. The types were (1) drug therapy, using imipramine, a common antidepressant medication; (2) cognitive therapy; (3) interpersonal therapy, in which patients were taught to build a better social network; and (4) clinical management, which was little more than a doctor's interested concern for the patient, plus a placebo, or dummy pill. The last method was almost as effective as the others. Patients were seen regularly for twenty to thirty minutes by a physician who offered no formal psychotherapy but showed concern for the patient's ups and downs, sympathetic curiosity, and "watchful waiting." Evidently, it is not so important what method one uses as it is to show consistent interest and compassion for depressed people.

Our attitude toward people determines to a great extent how they react to us. Lou Tice, founder of the Pacific Institute in Seattle, says, "You may not get what you *want* in life, but you will get what you *expect.*" If you expect your customers to treat you as a second-class citizen because you're in sales, if you expect that they're going to run down your product and tell you your prices are too high, then they probably will. On the other hand, if you expect them to be well-intentioned people who need to buy your product and want to trust you, then that's probably who they will be with you. Expectation is the key.

On an airplane recently I made the mistake of admitting to the woman next to me that I'm in the psychology business. "Oh," she said brightly. "You're just the one I want to talk to. My husband is completely dissociated from reality." For the next hour she told me how much she hated Los Angeles and how she was trying to get her husband to make the break and move with her to Ketchum, Idaho. She hated LA's smog, and she hated its culture. The crime was disgraceful, the traffic was awful, nobody was friendly, everyone was out to cheat you, and the people moving into her neighborhood were riffraff.

She was a nice lady, and I hope she'll be happy in Ketchum, but I've noticed that those who are miserable in

LA are usually miserable in Ketchum as well. On the other hand, those who believe that love is the greatest power we possess find things to enjoy in the people around them regardless of the locale.

An Enlightened View of Mistakes

A woman I admire very much has a kitchen uncluttered by the traditional signs and slogans, but she does have this motto over the sink: "Love forgets mistakes." Optimists do not harbor grudges or hoard memories of previous wrongs. This is not only because they have a high view of the human race but also because they have a distinctive way of thinking about the nature of mistakes. They see them as a spring-board to learning.

The manager of an IBM project that lost $10 million before it was scrapped was called into a meeting at the corporate office.

"I suppose you want my resignation?" he said.

"Resignation nothing!" replied his boss. "We've just spent $10 million *educating* you."

An Optimistic Attitude Makes You More Attractive

We have been discussing the topic of love at more length than any other for the simple reason that one can never become an optimist without it. But if you become more optimistic when you love more, the other side of the circle is that you will find more love when you are more optimistic.

A letter recently came from a patient I had not seen in several years.

"Remember me?" she wrote. "I was the one who couldn't hold a man."

I remembered her well. She was a striking young woman.

"I don't have any trouble attracting men," she had begun at her first session. "In fact, it's just the opposite. But after three or four weeks the relationship begins to go sour. It's happened so often I know it must be me."

As our sessions progressed, it was obvious that her attitude *did* drive men away. She had been traumatized in her youth and had many reasons to be cynical and hostile. But it was easy to see why men drifted off after a few dates, despite her good looks.

As we talked, she said that in order to be successful with men, she knew she would have to change her disposition, but she had little hope that it was possible (typical for a pessimist!). Three years earlier she had been in extensive therapy, during which she delved into her unconscious and tried the traditional ways of getting to one's neuroses. This time we agreed not to worry much about the unconscious causes of her depression and bleak outlook. I introduced her to some of the exercises used by the cognitive therapists and gave her specific homework each week for modifying her patterns of thought. The idea was to work on changing her outward behavior, assuming that when she began to act lovable, she would feel more lovable. She was very motivated to move ahead, worked hard every session, and in a surprising amount of time became a smiling, bright-eyed woman.

As often happens, after ending therapy, she drifted away, and I did not know her whereabouts for several years. So I eagerly read on.

"You'll be glad to know," she wrote, "that Tom and I have been married three years now, and so far, so good. We just had an eight-pound baby, and I can't imagine that life could be better."

In his famous poem to love, Saint Paul tells us that there are three things that have abiding worth: faith, hope, and love. There is no question that for the construction and maintenance of the optimistic spirit we must have all three. But Paul is right about which of these building blocks is most important. It is love.

If you keep on saying things are going to be bad, you have a good chance of being a prophet.

ISAAC SINGER

12 □ Your Talk Affects Your State of Mind

In their best-selling book, *In Search of Excellence,* Thomas J. Peters and Robert H. Waterman, Jr., reported on the characteristics of the best-managed corporations in America. One of their discoveries about these high-morale companies was that "good news swapping" was common. Top executives understood the value of taking time to relate a favorable anecdote or pass on an encouraging statistic.

It is a significant characteristic in every optimist:

☐ *Optimists like to swap good news.*

For five years Steve Bow was senior vice-president of the Metropolitan Life Insurance Company, in charge of thirteen states and five thousand people in Metropolitan's western head office and territory. During those five years the average branch office almost doubled in size, managers and account representatives doubled their incomes, and total sales rose 235 percent. How do you turn around a large section of a company like that? Bow says that one of their major actions taken was to "create and maintain an atmosphere of success. We talked about our successes and we minimized our failures. We created a belief that things were going in the right direction."

At business meetings it is natural to spend the majority of the time dealing with problems; eventually the only reason you meet is to discuss difficulties. That is a serious tactical error. One of the most important reasons for business teams to meet is to fuel one another's enthusiasm. You meet to multiply your energies. As embers need to touch one another to catch on fire, so highly motivated people need to rub shoulders with other such people in order to operate at their highest level. They like to talk about one another's progress and congratulate one another, and when there have been successes, they like to figure out what caused them so they can be repeated.

The decision to be a repeater of good news can turn around a family or a marriage as well. I once knew a man who was married to a stunningly attractive woman, then left her for a woman in his office whom people described as "a little frumpy." It was a reverse stereotype, for rather than leaving his wife to have an affair with some sexy, younger woman, he was doing the opposite.

I was appointed to "talk some sense into him," but I didn't get very far. The reason for his move, he explained, was simple. He couldn't handle his wife's negativism any longer. Their evenings were spent listening to her complaints. When they were in a restaurant, she was constantly critical. He never did anything right. Eventually this black cloud became too much for him.

His new love, he said, might not be any great looker, but she loved him without qualification, "and when she opens her mouth it's usually to say something cheerful," he said. "If I meet her after work for dinner, she tells me what went on at her office during the day. If something went wrong or irritated her at work, she doesn't hide that; but mostly we talk about the good things that happened, a funny thing someone said, her appreciation for some quality in one of her colleagues."

He went on, "Let me give you an illustration of what she's like. We'll be eating dinner at a coffee shop, and my inclination will be to say, 'Well, this place is no Gennaro's, is it?' But instead of a cynical remark like that she'll say, 'You know, for a coffee shop, this place is not bad, is it?'"

Complaining as Habit

Corporations occasionally ask me to work with their low-producing managers and salespersons, the people who are failing, but whom they'd like to reclaim. As I sit with these men and women and listen to their conversation, I'm always struck by how pessimistic and cynical their talk is. One might say, "Of course, they're negative; they know they're in trouble in their company." But I suspect that it may have worked the other way—that one reason they became losers was their habit of negative talk. At some point they evidently got into the habit of commenting on bad circumstances, the bad working conditions, the bad state of their business. Maybe it originally got them some sympathy and attention, or maybe they picked up the habit from other workers. In any event, they became negative, dour people, and their work suffered.

Do we have to be at the mercy of such programming? Certainly not. One of my friends is a savvy salesperson and one of the most cheerful, enthusiastic persons I know. Yet she grew up with parents who were constantly bickering and fighting. Her father was a brilliant man, but a curmudgeon who hated his work and did not get along with people.

The saleswoman says, "I loved my dad and felt sorry for him, but I saw how much misery he caused at home. I determined I would not be like him, that I would laugh a lot, find things to believe in and be enthusiastic about, and try to have some good news to pass on to the people I meet."

I asked my friend if that meant she was so optimistic that she never felt defeated or discouraged.

"Oh no," the woman replied. "I get down just like everybody. But I refuse to stay down. I don't let those disappointments find any permanent niche in my brain. And the way I try to control it is by my choice of what I say to the people around me. It's amazing how quickly you can pull yourself out of depression by choosing a cheerful topic and discussing that for a few minutes, and suddenly you find that your mood has shifted."

How to Cope with the Complainer

When I do management seminars on how to motivate one's staff, I'm often told by someone at the coffee break, "What you say is well and good, but it'll never work with my staff. They're the most stubborn group of pessimists in the world, and nothing I do can get them to stop complaining."

How *should* we react when others are negative? One of the best techniques is what one manager calls benign neglect. It works very well in changing a negative tone in a conversation, and it is a technique that the best motivators and leaders have used for centuries. A successful salesman told me that when he is making a presentation to clients he tries to keep a high energy level throughout the conversation. He sits forward as they talk. He uses lots of positive body language to show that he's listening carefully, nodding, connecting with the clients in many nonverbal ways, chiming in with comments to encourage them to keep talking about their needs. "But then," he said, "if they interrupt with objections or start telling me the reasons they can't buy, I don't try to answer every objection. In many instances, I just get quiet. I stop nodding and listen quietly, without responding. Then, when there's an opportunity, I move back into talking about the benefits of my product."

The same technique can work with complainers. When they are telling how terrible the world is and how crooked all the politicians are and how hypocritical the churches are, it's not productive to try to argue every point. If, like the salesman, we simply grow silent for a while, the direction of the conversation may shift very soon.

Choosing from Your Mind's Data Base

Cheerful people do not allow their minds to wander long among unpleasant facts and memories. They treat the mind like a computer from which they pull up certain files, and they keep looking through the files until they find something good to discuss.

My new neighbor, Everett Wood, is eighty-six, and has lived in his home here in Glendale, California, for almost fifty years. Our house is part of a new development that was, to the consternation of the neighbors, carved into the hillsides above them. Since our home was up the hill from Everett's, I didn't expect him to be particularly friendly when we moved in. The day we met I said, "Mr. Wood, if I were you, I don't think I'd appreciate all these newcomers spoiling your scenery."

He looked off into the distance, then smiled a warm, welcoming smile and said, "Well, change is a good thing, and at night now we look up at your house with all the lights burning, and it looks very friendly." Then he went on to talk about other things with enthusiasm. It was as if he had scanned a range of possible comments until he found a positive one — the friendly lights — and that was the one he chose to pull out and put into words.

Such choices come to us every day. At breakfast we can, if we wish, choose to articulate thoughts such as "Well, he didn't take out the trash — again"; "What a mess that room of hers is"; "Can you believe he parked the car behind ours in the driveway after we've told him all these times?" Or we can say, "Tom and I are going to have lunch today. I always look forward to seeing him."

What we discuss with other people has a significant influence not only on their moods but ours, because when we take a feeling — good or bad — out of our data bank and put it into words, we give that emotion a life of its own. It may have been shifting, changing, in flux within our minds. But once we label it with words, it takes on a much more permanent form, and it can have a remarkably long life.

137

Storytelling and the Communication of Good News

"Good design sells" is an article of faith at Herman Miller, Inc., which has been making good money with good design for years. Among other distinctions, its 1956 Eames lounge chair is exhibited in the New York Museum of Modern Art, and Miller is always one of the top-ranked furniture makers on *Fortune*'s list of most-admired corporations.

What made Herman Miller such a successful company? Some of the secrets are in a small book entitled *Leadership Is an Art* by Max DePree, president at Herman Miller for many years. He tells the following story:

> One of the giants in Herman Miller's history was a man named Jim Eppinger. Jim was the sales manager of the company through the thirties and forties and, in particular, during our transition from making good-quality, traditional copies of furniture to learning how to sell the revolutionary new designs of Rhode and Nelson and Eames. Those were tough years, really tough years that only a few people still understand.
>
> Once I sat in on a luncheon with my father and Jim Eppinger—these two old cronies who had really made the company survive during the Depression. They were talking with a sense of humor and nostalgia, about some of the difficulties of the early days and, in particular, the Depression.
>
> My father recalled for Jimmy a time they had been together at Jim's home in New Jersey during Christmastime and mentioned how much he was aware that Jim's family had no Christmas tree nor any gifts. Dad knew it was because the company did not have enough money to pay the sales commissions that were due.

Dad mentioned that Jim probably didn't remember that time, but it was very real to my father because he felt it was his fault that Jim's family would have no Christmas. But Jim said, "I remember that evening as if it were yesterday, because for Marian and me it was one of the highlights of our lives."

And my dad, surprised, said, "How could that possibly be?"

Jim said, "Well, don't you remember? That was the night you give me the New York territory. It was the greatest opportunity I've ever had."

That is a wonderful story in itself, but it is interesting for what it tells about the psychology of a successful leader like DePree. Chances are DePree has told that story over and over to the people within his company. Such tribal storytelling, as DePree calls it, is as important in families and churches as it is in a company like Herman Miller.

How to Make Yourself Sick

What we choose to talk about has a lot to do with our health. For instance, the more we talk about how bad we feel, the sicker we usually get. For some of us, if we wake up feeling the onset of a fever, we let everyone at breakfast know the peril we're in. When we arrive at the office, we say, "Somebody please get me some coffee. I'm feeling terrible this morning." At the next opportunity to get someone to listen, we say, "Must be coming down with the flu. This is the worst headache I've had in years." The more we talk about how we feel, the sicker we get. The effect is deleterious not only for ourselves but also for the people around us.

There is an old story, perhaps apocryphal, about the employees of a furniture factory in Michigan who would play an initiation prank on new workers. On some agreed-upon day they began to drop by the newcomer's machine, one by one, and say, "Joe, you don't look so good today. Are you feeling sick?" At first he would protest that he felt fine, but all morning different people would tell him how bad he looked, that he should sit down and rest. Usually the poor man would go home sick by noon.

We have remarkable suggestive powers in our choice of conversational topics.

Repression Versus Selection

Part of our difficulty with this topic is that the pop psychologists have taught us to worship our emotions. We have been told that we all have feelings, that we are not responsible for them, and that the best thing to do is to express them. According the Freud, the repression of emotion is the source of all neurosis.

To some extent, Freud was right. We have many feelings that bubble up from our unconscious, and it is a mistake to try to live as if they were not there. But often the more we talk about certain negative feelings, the more we reinforce them, and that gives them credence and grants them power.

Let's take a couple of examples. Suppose you come home tired, discouraged by several things that went wrong during the day. If you spend the evening grousing about how tired you are and how bad things are at the office, you make those around you miserable and you probably make yourself more tired.

Home should be a place where you can put up your feet, let down your hair, and not have to pretend. So if you're tired and angry at your boss, it's good to be able to say so, knowing your family will accept you—and your feelings—as you are. But don't make the family miserable by coming back to the same joyless topics all evening. Having told them your troubles, go on to other things.

Our daughter Donna, a consummate optimist, came home from a date one night recently, disappointed because the movie theater's projector broke and the manager had to give everyone passes to another showing. Had some people been in Donna's place, they would have spent the next fifteen minutes railing at the theater for its slovenly management, criticizing them for having no back-up equipment, telling anyone who would listen that it was a rotten trick. But not Donna. After saying that she and her boyfriend were disappointed, she said, "But what we saw of the movie was *very* good."

In almost every situation, it is possible to give the conversation an optimistic spin.

The essence of genius is knowing
what to overlook.

WILLIAM JAMES

13 □ The Art of Accepting What Cannot Be Changed

One might make a case that malcontents have made most of the world's great inventions and discoveries. "Show me a thoroughly satisfied man—and I will show you a failure," Thomas Edison once wrote. So there is something to be said for discontent.

But most of us go too far. We waste much of our lives kicking at frustrations, regretting the way things have turned out, beating our heads against the wall unnecessarily, when the wise thing would be to learn the art of acceptance. There is an art to putting the past behind us and accepting the world as it is rather than trying to improve it all at once.

So the twelfth characteristic is:

☐ *Optimists accept what cannot be changed.*

As in most things, balance is essential; yet the balance between tenacity and submission is not easy to keep. At sales meetings, motivational speakers often wax eloquent on the virtues of perseverance. The assumption seems to be that if you never quit and if you believe hard enough for long enough, you'll eventually hit pay dirt. Often they tell stories about an oil explorer who quit drilling only a few feet short of a great basin of oil, or a gold miner who dug four thousand feet into a mountainside, then stopped tunneling just short of a vein of gold. "If he had only dug *another fifty feet*," the speaker will say.

Just what are such stories supposed to mean? That we should *never* give up? That when we've drilled four thousand feet unsuccessfully, we should go on to twenty thousand? Or a hundred thousand? There is such a thing as cutting your losses and going on to other projects that hold more hope. W. C. Fields once said, "If at first you don't succeed, try again. If the second time you still do not succeed, try once again. But if the third time you do not succeed, quit. There's no use being a fool about it."

145

The Art of Contentment

"Thou shalt not covet," reads one of the Ten Commandments, and most of my patients could enjoy their days more if they obeyed that rule. They think they would be happy if they were someone else, if they had someone else's job or were married to someone else. But contentment often comes from the conscious act of acceptance. Buffy Sainte-Marie, a full-blooded Cree Indian and a successful folksinger, once said, "I wanted to be a blonde. My ambition was first to be a cheerleader and then an airline stewardess—like the average girl. Then I realized that as the average girl I was a failure. So I decided to be myself."

Tilden Edwards tells of the important symbolism to him of a ceramic sea otter on his desk, a gift from his wife:

> The otter is floating on its back, eating an abalone
> from a cracked shell: an alluring scene I have wit-
> nessed many times along the California coast. . . .
> The otter is a reminder of much that I have come to
> appreciate about life in these last few years: the way
> we are held up when we attentively relax into it; the
> buoyancy this experience and trust give us; the great
> energy available then to put into work and caring,
> yet work and caring that has a playful, simple edge.

Note how different such an approach is from that of people who are forever complaining that they can't get a cab, or that the traffic is heavy, or that it is raining. Some will say, "Why is it raining all the time? It shouldn't be raining! The weatherman didn't predict this. It's June! This is not fair! It didn't rain last June!"

Or consider the freeway traffic. The worse it gets, the more irritable we get, honking at people who cut us off, muttering that we'll never make our next appointment. This general ill humor spreads even more discourtesy up and down the freeway. One psychologist says that well-functioning people say to themselves, "The traffic will be heavy until it's no longer heavy. What is, is." So they relax in their cars, take in the sights, and listen to music.

A teacher whose name I have forgotten has a good differentiation between psychotics and neurotics. You ask psychotics what is two times two and they may say nineteen, or twenty-six, whatever comes into their heads. Those people must be protected. When you ask neurotics what is two times two, they say, "It's four, but I can't stand it! Why does it always have to be four? It's so boring! It's four all the time! Why wasn't I asked for input on that decision? Why can't it be five once in a while?"

When faced with a difficult situation, we can ask ourselves, "What can I do to change this situation?" If there is nothing, we can elect to shut it out, to concentrate on things to be enjoyed. In a bookstore recently I noticed a book title that I would like as a sign to hang on my office wall. It would be there for my patients, but I am the one who needs it most. It reads, "All you can do is all you can do, but all you can do is enough."

Flexibility as a Virtue

Happy people know how to adapt. They are nimble, they learn new things, they adjust. For instance, few of us have the sort of life we initially thought we wanted. And thank God we don't! Some people make themselves miserable by being so stubborn about their plans for the future. When they have to take new directions, they resist and rebel. "Things are not the way they used to be," they complain, or "This is not the way things were supposed to work out."

The happiest and most successful people are those who are fleet-footed, who are eager to learn new ways, who adapt to new systems when the old ones do not work. When one career path fails, they cheerfully learn a new way of earning a living. When their marriage ends, they're able to adjust to being alone or to a new marriage. When people frustrate them and they see that these people are never going to change, they accept them the way they are and relax.

As they say in Alcoholics Anonymous: "Change what you can and accept what you can't."

The mind is its own place, and in itself
Can make a heaven of hell, a hell of heaven.

JOHN MILTON

14 □ Transformational Power

Throughout these pages I have been saying that we have a great deal of control over the attitude we take toward the world around us and, consequently, a great deal of power over that world. Of all living creatures, only human beings have the capacity to alter their destiny by altering their attitudes.

Harry Emerson Fosdick wrote about growing up in upstate New York, where one summer day his mother sent him out to pick a quart of raspberries. "I dragged my feet in rebellion," he says, "and the can was filling very slowly. Then a new idea came: it would be fun to pick two quarts of raspberries and surprise her. I had so interesting a time picking two quarts to the utter amazement of the household, and they never forgot it. But alas, I have often forgotten the philosophy of it: we can change any situation by changing our attitude toward it. Nobody ever finds life worth living. One always has to *make* it worth living."

Is Pessimism More Realistic?

At the beginning of this book I said that no one wants to be a pessimist, but there are those who claim to be pessimists simply because they want to be "realistic." Indeed, some bright intellectuals have charged that when the world contains molesters and murderers, and when something as terrible as the Holocaust can occur in our century, it is simpleminded to take an optimistic view of the world.

It is a question we ought to consider. Certainly we would be simpleminded if we attempted to live as if our world contained no pain or injustice. But the practical optimists of the world rarely lead lives untouched by suffering. To the contrary, they often know great hardship. When Saint Paul, for instance, wrote his remarkable letter about joy to the Philippians, he was in a Roman jail, awaiting—so far as he knew—execution.

Dr. Viktor Frankl is a writer whose thoughts about the Holocaust have particular poignancy because he was there. His book, *Man's Search for Meaning*, was written as he looked back at almost three years in Auschwitz, Dachau, and other such camps during World War II. "We wondered," he says, "at what caused some men to survive and others to perish. It was an apparent paradox that some persons of a less hardy makeup often seemed to survive camp life better than those of a robust nature." The explanation, he discovered, had to do with the state of their minds. Here is Frankl's eloquent comment on those years:

> The experiences of camp life show that man does have a choice of action. There were enough examples, often of a heroic nature, which proved that apathy could be overcome, irritability suppressed. Man *can* preserve a vestige of spiritual freedom, of independence of mind, even in such terrible conditions of psychic and physical stress.

> We who lived in concentration camps can remember the men who walked through the huts comforting others, giving away their last piece of bread. They may have been few in number, but they offer sufficient proof that everything can be taken from a man but one thing: the last of the human freedoms — to choose one's attitude in any given set of circumstances, to choose one's own way.

When Frankl talks about the freedom to choose one's attitude, even in such horrible depravity as a concentration camp, he is describing what is perhaps the clearest evidence that we have some of the Divine in us. This ability to convert evil, to turn suffering into growth, to take tragic aspects of our existence and transform them with the power of an optimistic view propelled by love — that is evidence of awesome power.

We may not live in concentration camps, but similar choices await us. We have the freedom to choose between evil and good, between suicide and life, between hate and love, between immediate gratification and long-range goals. If we wish, we can opt for the cynical, pessimistic view of this world. Or we can take the position of hope, which is stubborn enough to believe that the best is yet to be. That choice—that choice of attitude—is ours.

Notes

Preface

Studies of optimists (page 1): The relationship between attitude and health is a hotly debated topic of research for both psychologists and physicians. Martin E. P. Seligman, a research psychologist at the University of Pennsylvania, is a pioneer in these studies. See his forthcoming *Learned Optimism,* to be published by Alfred A. Knopf, Inc. As we shall see later, it is not always easy to distinguish between cause and effect in these studies, and some of the claims of mind cures for medical problems have been exaggerated. But the cumulative evidence is nevertheless inescapable: A positive point of view leads to enhanced success in almost every endeavor.

Pessimists (2): I do not dispute that our personal histories influence the way we see the world nor deny that some of us are born with what Hippocrates called melancholy dispositions.

There is now little question that some types of depression are inherited or have chemical causes. Such endogenous depression seems to come out of the thin air and is not tied to any outward events in one's life. One variety, for instance, the bipolar or manic-depressive type, afflicts three million Americans and appears to be entirely hereditary. This endogenous depression (as distinguished from reactive depression, which is triggered by some event) often requires medical treatment and will be less amenable to the techniques outlined here than the reactive type. But the worst thing we can do is to surrender to depression because it is "chemical" or "runs in the family." If some of us cannot eliminate depression from our lives, there are many things we can do to stave it off, to diminish it, to mitigate it.

Books and change of outlook (3): Recent studies show that personal growth books can be quite helpful for depressed persons. Two self-help books, *Control Your Depression* by Peter Lewisohn and *Feeling Good* by David Burns, were given to forty-five moderately depressed persons. They were asked to spend four weeks reading the books and were tested afterward. More than 60 percent showed a significant improvement. In a comparison group of men and women with similar depression who did not get the books during the study, the improvement rate in the same period was only about 20 percent (Forrest Scogin, Christine Jamison, and Kimberly Gochneaur, "Comparative Efficacy of Cognitive and Behavioral Bibliotherapy for Mildly and Moderately Depressed Older Adults," *Journal of Consulting and Clinical Psychology,* June 1989, pp. 403–7).

Chapter 1

Churchill, speech (7): Martin Gilbert, *Winston S. Churchill* (Boston: Houghton Mifflin, 1983), 7:468.

Bennis and Nanus (9): Warren Bennis and Burt Nanus, *Leaders,* Perennial Library Edition (New York: Harper & Row, 1985), p. 69. See also Warren Bennis's excellent book, *On Becoming a Leader* (Reading, MA: Addison-Wesley, 1989).

Odyssey (9): Homer, *The Odyssey,* trans. E. V. Rieu (Baltimore: Penguin Books, 1946), Book 1, p. 30.

Edison, experiments (10): Charles Edison, "My Most Unforgettable Character," *Reader's Digest*, December 1961, p. 174.

Kelsey (11): Morton Mintz, *Washington Post,* July 15, 1962, p. 1.

Sinclair Lewis (12): Charlie Rice in *This Week* Magazine. Quoted by *Reader's Digest,* July 1964, p. 117.

Bush (13): Time, January 23, 1989, p. 25.

C. S. Lewis, appearance (14): From a letter to John S. A. Ensor dated March 31, 1944. Quoted in Griffin, *Clive Staples Lewis.*

C. S. Lewis, love (14): From a letter to Alan Richard Griffiths dated September 24, 1957. Quoted in William Griffin, *Clive Staples Lewis* (San Francisco: Harper & Row, 1986), pp. 389–90.

C. S. Lewis, wife's death (15): Quoted in Griffin, *Clive Staples Lewis,* p. 422.

C. S. Lewis, anger (15): C. S. Lewis, *A Grief Observed* (San Francisco: Harper & Row, 1961), p. 43.

Edison's fire (16): Edison, "My Most Unforgettable Character," p. 177.

Pollock (17): Channing Pollock, *The Adventures of a Happy Man* (New York: Thomas Y. Crowell, 1939).

Kushner (18): Harold S. Kushner, *When All You've Ever Wanted Isn't Enough* (New York: Summit Books, 1986), pp. 162–68.

Hill (18): Napoleon Hill, *Think and Grow Rich* (New York: Fawcett Crest, 1960), p. 32.

Chapter 2

Jesus (24): John 9:7, Mark 3:5, Luke 5:24.

Carlyle (25): Fred Kaplan, *Thomas Carlyle: A Biography* (Ithaca: Cornell University Press, 1983), p. 218.

Franklin (25): Benjamin Franklin, *The Autobiography and Other Writings* (New York: Bantam Books, 1982), p. 118.

Goethe (26): Johann Wolfgang von Goethe, *Faust,* trans. John Anster 1:303 (New York: Frederick A. Stokes, 1890) p. 30.

Study of perfectionism (27): David D. Burns, "The Perfectionist's Script for Self-Defeat," *Psychology Today,* November 1980, pp. 34–52.

Caleb and Joshua (28): Numbers 13–14.

Woodhull (28): Ronni Sandroff, "The Manager Who Never Says Never," *Working Woman,* December 1989, pp. 90–94, 124.

Rabbi's Ty Cobb story (30): For this anecdote I'm indebted to Robert Fulghum, *All I Really Need to Know I Learned in Kindergarten* (New York: Villard Books, 1989), pp. 165–66.

Chapter 3

Learned helplessness (35): Martin E. P. Seligman, *Helplessness: On Depression, Development and Death* (San Francisco: W. H. Freeman, 1975).

Roosevelt (36): Harold E. Kohn, *Through the Valley* (Grand Rapids: W. B. Eerdmans Publishing, 1957).

Antidepression room (37): E. S. Taulbee and H. W. Wright, "A Psychosocial-Behavioral Model for Therapeutic Intervention," *Current Topics in Clinical and Community Psychology,* ed. Charles D. Speilberger (Orlando, FL: Academic Press, 1971).

Sanford (37): John A. Sanford, *Ministry Burnout* (New York: Paulist Press, 1982), p. 23.

Welch (38): Stratford P. Sherman, "The Mind of Jack Welch," *Fortune,* March 27, 1989, p. 39.

Individual's control of future (39): There is some evidence that pessimists are, in certain situations, better transducers of reality than optimists. Timothy M. Osberg, Lauren B. Alloy, and Lyn Y. Abramson have all found in their studies that nondepressed persons see things less realistically and are a little out of touch with reality in the benign direction. Pessimists are "sadder but wiser," says Martin E. P. Seligman. "If you want someone to invest in the stock market for you, find someone who is mildly depressed." But these findings are not surprising. The pessimist is interested in the status quo and sees things as they are. The optimist is more interested in the future and sees things as they could be.

Lincoln (40): Benjamin P. Thomas, *Abraham Lincoln* (New York: The Modern Library, 1968).

Chapter 4

Schweitzer (46): Albert Schweitzer, *The Words of Albert Schweitzer* (New York: New Market Publishing, 1984), p. 60.

Nouwen (49): Henri J. M. Nouwen, *The Road to Daybreak* (New York: Doubleday, 1988), pp. 19, 28.

Hanh (51): Thich Nhat Hanh, *Being Peace* (Berkeley: Parallax Press, 1987), pp. 4, 9.

Edwards (51): Tilden Edwards, *All God's Children* (Nashville: Abingdon Press, 1982), pp. 109–110.

Sculley (52): "John Sculley on Sabbatical," *Fortune,* March 27, 1989, pp. 79–80.

Chapter 5

Lincoln's melancholy (57): Benjamin P. Thomas, *Abraham Lincoln* (New York: The Modern Library, 1968), pp. 88, 133.

Hansel (61): Tim Hansel, *You Gotta Keep Dancin'* (Elgin, IL, D. C. Cook, 1985).

Larson (63): Bruce Larson, *The One and Only You* (Waco, TX: Word Books, 1974), pp. 79–80.

Personalizing (65): There is an obvious danger here. We all know people who avoid responsibility by crediting their failures to external forces when in fact they are creating their own problems. If we see all failures as coming from external circumstances and all successes as coming from internal powers, we are deluded. As in most things, balance is the key. Seligman is the first to point this out and says that the internal-external criterion is not nearly so important for determining optimism as the global-specific and permanent-temporary questions.

Chapter 6

Saint Paul (71): Philippians 4:8.

Nevelson (73): Natalie S. Bober, *Breaking Tradition* (New York: Atheneum, 1984), p. 139.

Rayburn (73): D. B. Hardeman, "Unseen Side of the Man They Called Mr. Speaker," *Life,* Dec. 1, 1961, p. 21.

Salk (74): Guideposts, February 1983, pp. 38–39.

Hanh (78): Thich Nhat Hanh, *Being Peace,* pp. 91, 3–4, respectively.

Chapter 7

Visualization by athletes (82): Stephen M. Kosslyn, "Stalking the Mental Image," *Psychology Today,* May 1985, p. 27.

Salesman (82): Arthur Gordon, "Where Success Comes From," *Reader's Digest,* July 1960, p. 43.

Palmer (83): "Making Leaders at Wharton," *Fortune,* October 24, 1988, p. 66.

Coffee (88): Gerald Coffee, *Beyond Survival* (New York: G. P. Putnam's Sons, 1990).

Chapter 8

Sills (91): "Beverly Sills: The Fastest Voice Alive," *Time,* November 22, 1971, p. 81.

James (91): William James, *Talks to Teachers on Psychology* (London: Longmans, Green, 1907), p. 201.

Kennedy (92): Cleveland Amory, "When Faith Is Triumphant," *Parade Magazine,* July 3, 1984, p. 4.

Cousins (95): Norman Cousins, *Anatomy of an Illness as Perceived by the Patient* (New York: Bantam Books, 1979). Some newspaper accounts distorted Cousins's position. At no time did he advocate laughter as a *substitute* for traditional medical attention. See his *Head First* (New York: E. P. Dutton, 1989).

A cheerful heart (95): Proverbs 17:22.

Schweitzer, Cousins (95): Norman Cousins, *Anatomy of an Illness,* p. 82.

Fry (95): William F. Fry, Jr., *Insight,* May 25, 1987, p. 59. For further physiology of humor see William F. Fry, Jr.'s "Humor, Physiology, and the Aging Process," in *Humor and Aging,* ed. Lucille Nahemow, Kathleen A. McCluskey-Fawcett, and Paul E. McGhee (Orlando, FL: Academic Press, 1986), pp. 81–98.

Hanser (97): Richard Hanser, "The Other Abraham Lincoln," *The Lion,* January, 1952, pp. 15–16.

Cassidy (97): "Precious Spikenard," *Catholic New Times of Toronto,* 1985, quoted by Henri J. M. Nouwen, *The Road to Daybreak: A Spiritual Journey* (New York: Doubleday, 1988), p. 21.

New York Philharmonic (98): George R. Marek, "Take Music Instead of Miltown," *The Art of Living* (New York: Berkeley Books, 1980), pp. 144–45.

Thayer (99): See Robert E. Thayer, *The Biopsychology of Mood and Arousal* (New York: Oxford University Press, 1989).

Health and optimism (100): Christopher Peterson, "Explanatory Style as a Risk Factor for Illness," *Cognitive Therapy and Research* 12 (1988): 117–30. Christopher Peterson and Martin E. P. Seligman, "Explanatory Style and Illness," *Journal of Personality* 55, no. 2 (1987): 237–65. Christopher Peterson, Martin E. P. Seligman, and George E. Valliant, "Pessimistic Explanatory Style as a Risk Factor for Physical Illness: A Thirty-Five-Year Longitudinal Study," *Journal of Personality and Social Psychology* 55 (1988): 23–27. *Cancer and attitude:* H. S. Greer, T. Morris, and K. W. Pettingale, "Psychological Response to Breast Cancer: Effect on Outcome," *Lancet* 2 (1979): 785–87. K. W. Pettingale, T. Morris, S. Greer, and J. S. Haybittle, "Mental Attitudes to Cancer: An Additional Prognostic Factor," *Lancet* 8 (1985): 750. See also Sandra M. Levy, "Behavior as a Biological Response Modifier: The Psychoimmunoendocrine Network and Tumor Immunology," *Behavioral Medicine Abstracts* 6, no. 1 (1985): 1–4, and S. Levy, R. Herberman, M. Lippman, and T. d'Angelo, "Correlation of Stress Factors with Sustained Depression of Natural Killer Cell Activity and Predicted Prognosis in Patients with Breast Cancer," *Journal of Clinical Oncology* 5 (1987): 348–53.

The New England Journal of Medicine published an important article with an opposing view on this subject. A study by B. R. Cassileth and others found that patients with advanced cancer who had positive attitudes fared no better than those who did not. In an accompanying editorial Dr. Marcia Angell stated: "It is time to acknowledge that our belief in disease as a direct reflection of mental state is largely folklore." This debate will not be ended for some time, but it is important to note that the Cassileth study was with advanced, high-risk malignant diseases, and she has since gone to some lengths to say that her studies do not rule out the effects of positive attitudes in the treatment of illness, but merely show that in advanced cancer, "biology overwhelms psychology." B. R. Cassileth, E. J. Lusk, D. S. Miller. L. L. Brown, and C. Miller, "Psychosocial Correlates of Survival in Advanced Malignant Disease," *New England Journal of Medicine* 312 (1985): 368–73.

James (101): William James, *Talks to Teachers on Psychology,* p. 201.

Chapter 9

Thomas, brain cells (106): Lewis Thomas, *The Medusa and the Snail* (New York: Viking, 1978), p. 157.

Thomas, warts (107): Lewis Thomas, *The Medusa and the Snail,* p. 79.

Lipsig (108): Wall Street Journal, June 12, 1989, Sec. A, pp. 1, 4.

Loren (109): Sophia Loren, *Women and Beauty* (New York: William Morrow, 1984), p. 218.

Chapter 10

Clark (113): Los Angeles Times, September 20, 1988, Pt. 4, p. 3.

Nin (113): Anaïs Nin, *The Four-Chambered Heart* (Chicago: Swallow Press, 1959), p. 48.

Anderson (113): Robert Anderson, *Solitaire/Double Solitaire* (New York: Random House, 1972) p. 32.

Durant, Byrd (114): June Callwood, "The One Sure Way to Happiness," *The Art of Living* (New York: Berkeley Books, 1980), p. 157.

Berkman (115): Paul Faulkner, *Making Things Right* (Fort Worth: Sweet Publishing, 1986), p. 155.

Love and angina pectoris (115): Maya Pines, "Psychological Hardiness," *Psychology Today,* December 1980, p. 43.

Towne (116): New York Times, November 27, 1988, Sec. H, p. 13.

Chapter 11

Williams, hostility (123): Redford Williams, M.D., *The Trusting Heart* (New York: Times Books, 1989), pp. 52, 68.

Williams, forgiveness (123): Redford Williams, M.D., *The Trusting Heart,* p. 195.

Fulghum (124): Robert Fulghum, *It Was on Fire When I Lay Down on It* (New York: Villard Books, 1989), pp. 46–47.

Stories and therapists (126): In his rich book, *The Call of Stories* (Boston: Houghton Mifflin, 1989), Harvard psychiatrist Robert Coles argues that psychotherapists could benefit from reading fiction. Our patients, he says, bring us their stories and hope that they can tell them well enough that we understand the truth of their lives.

Role of doctor (126): Much of the interpretation of this study remains to be done and debate about it will rage for years, as various schools of treatment fight for their turf. It should be noted that the placebo, benign as it was, may have generated positive expectations that contributed to the improvement, and it must also be noted that clinical management was not as helpful for severely depressed patients as other methods. For further study see Irene Elkin, Ph.D., and others, "National Institute of Mental Health Treatment of Depression Collaborative Research Program," *Archives of General Psychiatry* 46 (November 1989): 971–83.

Saint Paul, Love (130): 1 Corinthians 13:13 rsv.

Chapter 12

Thomas J. Peters and Robert H. Waterman, Jr., *In Search of Excellence* (New York: Harper & Row, 1982), p. 71.

DePree (138): Max DePree, *Leadership Is an Art* (New York: Doubleday, 1989), pp. 65–66.

Chapter 13

Edwards (146): Tilden Edwards, *Living Simply Through the Day* (New York: Paulist Press, 1977), p. 1.

Chapter 14

Frankl (152): Viktor E. Frankl, *Man's Search for Meaning,* 3rd ed. (New York: Touchstone Books, 1984), p. 65.

About the Author

Dr. Alan Loy McGinnis is a founder and director of Valley Counseling Center in Glendale, California, where a team of psychiatrists and therapists work together for the healing of the whole person.

Dr. McGinnis holds degrees from Princeton, Wheaton, Fuller, and Columbia. A family therapist, Dr. McGinnis has done extensive research on the dynamics of motivation and on techniques for resolving interpersonal conflicts. For that reason, Many *Fortune 500* companies use his services as a speaker and seminar leader for sales and management conferences.

A dynamic and humorous speaker, Dr. McGinnis has been the main-platform speaker for such organizations as the Million Dollar Round Table and National Tour Association. He has given seminars for companies such as IBM, Dow Chemical, Metropolitan Life, Coldwell Banker, ServiceMasters, Alexander Grant, CIGNA, Pacific Telephone, American Bankers Life, Paracelsus Health Care, and John Hancock.

Dr. McGinnis has published over fifty articles in national magazines including *Reader's Digest, The Saturday Evening Post, Guideposts, Cosmopolitan, Redbook, Good Housekeeping,* and *Ladies' Home Journal.* His first book *The Friendship Factor* is an international best-seller. Now in its twenty-eighth printing in the U.S., with more than one million copies in print, it has been translated into twelve languages. His other best-selling books include *The Romance Factor, Bringing Out the Best in People,* and *Confidence.*

Dr. McGinnis has been a guest on more than three hundred radio and TV shows in the United States and Canada and is a regular on several nationwide programs. He is married and has four children.